A CUP OF COMFORT®
for
Inspiration

Uplifting stories
that will
brighten your day

Edited by Colleen Sell

Avon, Massachusetts

For Daniel, my brother:
The captain of his own ship,
A beacon in the stormy sea.

Published by
Adams Media, a division of F+W Media, Inc.
57 Littlefield Street, Avon, MA 02322 U.S.A.
www.adamsmedia.com and *www.cupofcomfort.com*
ISBN 10: 1-4405-0499-7
ISBN 13: 978-1-4405-0499-0

Printed in the United States of America.

10 9 8 7 6 5 4 3 2 1

Library of Congress Cataloging-in-Publication Data
A cup of comfort for inspiration / edited by Colleen Sell.
p.   cm.
1. Conduct of life. I. Sell, Colleen.
BJ1597.C87 2003
158.1'28--dc21
2003008260

 # Acknowledgments

What a privilege it is to do work that is inspiring and interesting.

What a joy it is to work with kind and talented people.

What an honor it is to produce a work that brings comfort and cheer to so many.

For these blessings, I thank the staff of Adams Media, the authors whose stories appear in this book, and you, dear readers.

For their love and support, I thank my beloved husband, family, and friends.

For the gift of meaningful, enjoyable work, I thank my lucky stars.

Contents

Introduction vii

Angel Wings • Joyce Holt 1
Doll Cake • Sandy Keefe 6
Willed • Janice Lane Palko 11
A Bartender's Story • Kimberly Ripley 17
The Wonder of Now • Sue Vitou 24
Practical Magic • Christy Caballero 29
Incidental Kin • Brenda Fritsvold 34
Sweet Moments • Deborah H. Shouse 39
One Man and a Whole Lot of Somebodies
        • Beth Rothstein Ambler 44
Over the Hill • Marcia E. Brown 52
For the Love of Pixie • Leigh P. Rogers 58
The Picture on the Wall • Danielle R. Gibbings 62
To Hold and Behold • Adrian R. Ward 66
The Greatest Man I Hardly Knew • Jean Davidson 71
Strawberries • April Thompson 80
Sisters in Time • Amy Jenkins 87

Close Encounters of the Best Kind •
   Shery Ma Belle Arrieta 93

Roots for Sofia • Roberta B. Updegraff 99

I Won't Forget • William M. Barnes. 104

Ruthie's Run • John Forrest 111

Here and Now, If Not Always • Linda Sonna. 117

Reglar Feller • Charles Langley. 121

When All Is Said • Kim Zarzour. 126

The Salvation of Jan and Kurt • Nancy Gustafson 131

Power Ball of Love • Kelly L. Stone 138

Stopping Traffic • Gila Zalon 147

Prince of Paupers • Sharon Nesbit 153

So I Ask You • Nancy Scott 157

The Dollar Dance • Peggy MacKay 161

Give Your Heart Away • Michelle Peters 168

Keep Walking • Gina Daggett 177

The Connection • Marty Dodge 181

Passing the Halo • Anna Therien. 186

Corinna's Quilts • Susan B. Mitchell 194

The Journey of Jake and Dora • Valerie L. Merahn 200

With a Little Boost from My Friends • Binsey Coté 206

Errands of Honor • Mary Stripling 211

The Gloved Guitarist of Tossa de Mar • Joyce Stark. 219

Snow Angel • Dawn Goldsmith 224

Gotta Keep Paddling • Norma Lewis 229

The Last Long Wave Good-bye • Marjorie Rommel 237

Begin Again • Marcia Rudoff 246

Warm Hearts in a Cold Winter • Kathryn Gore 251

For Sura, Who Claimed Her Need to Be Touched •
    Barbara Whitby. 259
Recipe for Life • Nancy Baker 264
The Gift of Robin • Julie Clark Robinson. 269
Balance • Tracey Henry 272
Why I Carry a Bobolight • Greg Beatty 277
The Hall of Mirrors • Nan Leslie 285
Shuffle, Step • Judi Christy. 290
Gordon • Kimberly Ripley 296
Ambassadors Are Everywhere • Deborah H. Shouse 300
A Five-Dollar Bill • Harriet Cooper 304

Tell Your Story in the Next *Cup of Comfort!* 310
Contributors. 312
About the Editor 325

 Introduction

"There are two ways of spreading light: to be the candle or the mirror that reflects it."

—Edith Wharton

As we journey down the curvy, sometimes bumpy, path of life, most of us encounter people and experiences that inspire us to live more passionately and compassionately, with gratitude and generosity. These inspirations often come in times of trouble or uncertainty, as if in answer to a prayer. But they are just as likely to come unbidden during times of ease and abundance, reminding us of our blessings and of those less fortunate.

If we are paying attention, earth angels and divine interventions can help us over a hump or out of a slump. They can nudge us into taking positive action and lead us in the right direction. They can even transform our lives.

The miracle is that such inspirations are all around us, all the time . . . In the busy mom who brings casseroles to shut-ins and gathers canned goods for the local food bank. In the daughter of illiterate migrant workers who is the first in her family to attend college, on an academic achievement scholarship, and becomes a teacher. In the genuine smiles, and "Have a nice days," and dollar-for-a-paper-flower that pass between a bag lady and a businesswoman. In the friend who never forgets your milestones and always forgives your foibles.

Inspiration is in people who toe the line, yet never trade in their integrity. Who follow their dreams and the Golden Rule, with equal dedication. Who take care of themselves and give of themselves, generously and without fanfare.

Inspiration is in all the extraordinary "ordinary" people whose good deeds light the candles of compassion and whose passion for life reflects the potential in each of us.

Here are some of their stories.

May they brighten your path and inspire you to live with passion and compassion.

—*Colleen Sell*

Angel Wings

I answer the ringing phone. "Hello?"

"Hi, darlin, it's Patty. Haven't seen you in a while. How're you doing?"

It's not a rhetorical question. Patty knows I've been struggling recently with mood swings and insomnia as my hormones adjust to the approach of menopause.

"Pretty good today," I answer. "How about you?"

"Fine, as ever. Can you come over tomorrow around noon and change a phone number for me?"

"Sure."

She closes our conversation with her signature phrase: "Angel wings around you!"

Patty's friends number in the hundreds, and she keeps tabs on all of them. She's part of an interdenominational prayer circle that covers a great swath of western Washington. Just let slip one word about an ailment or a child having a crisis, and you know your name will get added to the list of folks needing mention in prayer.

As I walk down the block to Patty's house the next day, I feel a twinge of guilt. It should be me calling up to check on her, I tell myself. But life gets so hectic, and every day finds me rushing about to get all the needful things done.

Patty doesn't do any rushing around, although I joke with her about bundling her up in bubble wrap, sitting her on a skateboard, and pushing her down the street just to get some fresh air.

I walk into her room. Angels, wings spread, cover all the walls, beaming down on visitors. Angel paintings, angel sculptures, even a teddy bear with wings—they're all gifts from her friends. Beneath one of the angels is a framed certificate citing Patty's counseling credentials.

"Hi, darlin!" she says from her hospital bed. She's in her usual semireclining position.

I turn off her television.

"First, can you straighten out my right hand?" Patty asks.

I uncurl her fingers and tuck her hand back into place. The humming pump at the foot of the bed keeps the air mattress inflated.

"Now, raise the tray just a bit."

I circle around to her left side and adjust the

control on the tray's support post. On the tray sit the tools of Patty's life: a Bible; two phone books crammed with names and numbers of family, friends, and acquaintances; and a specialized telephone.

"See the slip of paper on the big black phone book?" she says. "That number needs to go in position five."

The telephone holds twenty programmed numbers. Patty can turn the phone on by blowing on a puffer switch positioned by her mouth. Then she waits until the blinking light cycles to the phone number she wants. Another puff on the switch and the phone dials out automatically. One of the programmed numbers summons the operator for calls to people not on the list.

I dig the telephone's instruction manual out of the drawer, find the right page, and punch the sequence of buttons to change the number for Patty's grown daughter, Jenny. Jenny's family has just moved to Boise, Idaho, where the job prospects are better and the cost of living lower than in the Seattle area.

"Jenny says there's a Mormon church on every corner. She says, 'Mom, the Mormons are gonna get me!'"

I laugh. Patty knows I'm Mormon. She and Jenny are Lutheran, and Patty's husband and young son are Catholic, but we have all the most important precepts in common. We all believe in God and angels and the power of prayer.

The phone rings. "Hello, hello!" Patty says. Her phone recognizes the command and turns on the speaker. A sad voice pipes up, and Patty goes into counselor mode. Who better to advise and comfort newly diagnosed multiple sclerosis patients than someone who knows the disease inside and out?

I look at family portraits on the bureau, while Patty talks with an acquaintance in distress. In one sense her world has shrunk to the four walls of her room, yet in another Patty's touch has spread to any-place a telephone can reach. Any place in our town, in our state, in our country.

"Angel wings around you!" she says at last and puffs to disconnect the phone.

"Would you check the calendar for me?" Patty asks.

I detach the calendar from its clip on the refrig-erator and bring it back to Patty's side.

"What birthdays are left this month?"

"Linda on the twenty-fifth," I say.

"Already done."

Another friend comes over regularly to address birthday cards. You can guess what greeting gets inscribed in each and every card!

"Matt on the twenty-seventh."

"Already done."

Someone else keeps Patty stocked up on greeting cards. Another friend does her Christmas shopping.

Each person who renders Patty some small service finds the deed a small thing in comparison to the ministration of love and care she gives in return. I often leave feeling humbled. If Patty can bear her trials with such grace and strength, how petty am I to complain over lesser problems?

"Gerene on the twenty-ninth."

"Already done."

Patty doesn't need the calendar off the fridge. She's got a better one in her head. Birthdays, anniversaries, names of children, details of the trials of family and close friends—she remembers them all. Her memory is nearly photographic.

Sure, she'd like the use of her arms and legs again. But since multiple sclerosis has shut down most of her body, Patty makes good use of what she has left: her voice, her mind, her heart.

I put the calendar back in place, and we chat for a while about my two grown daughters. When it's time to go, I turn on her television and say good-bye.

"Angel wings around you!" she calls after me.

Angel wings . . . invisible, unseen. As I close the door and walk outside, I feel them around me already. And I know that angel's name.

—Joyce Holt

Doll Cake

On a rainy winter morning, my daughter Allie and I scurried from the van into the house after dropping sister Shannon off at school. Cold and damp, we scrambled into a warm shower and dressed in snuggly fleece robes. A cup of hot chocolate was just the ticket, we agreed, padding to the kitchen in our fuzzy slippers. By some quirk of fate, the next two hours were amazingly free of medical appointments, therapy sessions, team meetings, and other commitments. Giggling like schoolgirls playing hooky, we curled up on our overstuffed sofa with a big pile of photo albums. While the rain pelted down on the windows, Allie and I exclaimed over pictures of a tiny Allie asleep in her crib and laughed at a print of a bathing suit–clad Allie smiling merrily from a bucket of soapy water as Dad washed the van.

Allie crowed joyfully when she flipped to the

page depicting her first birthday. Born with Down syndrome and severe heart defects, Allie had spent too much of her infancy in the intensive care unit at the university medical center. And there she was in a Polaroid shot, propped up in a highchair with tubes and monitor cables flowing from her body to nearby machines. Although she looked pale and fatigued, Allie flashed a winsome smile as she plunged both hands into the gooey frosting of her miniature cake.

Cakes have always been important to Allie. Chocolate cakes with fluffy white icing, round Bundt cakes glistening with sugary glaze, carrot cakes with cream cheese frosting, cupcakes topped with dollops of brightly colored icing—Allie loved them all. But most of all, Allie loved elaborately decorated cakes festooned with multicolored sprinkles, rainbows of icing, fairy tale figurines, tiny animals, paper umbrellas, lovely words inscribed in glistening frosting, sleek roses, and tiny silver balls. The more decorations, the better the cake.

Continuing on our evocative photo journey, Allie and I chuckled at pictures depicting long hours spent in front of a mirror with her speech therapist, hot summer afternoons playing Challenger Little League baseball with other children who had developmental delays, windy mornings at our therapeutic horseback riding program, and hard-earned accomplishments in occupational therapy.

Picking up a blue-flowered album, I opened to a snapshot taken when my oldest daughter Shannon was about six years old. Facing the camera with a gap-toothed grin, Shannon balanced a large plate precariously in both hands.

"Mommy," Allie exclaimed in amazement as she gazed at the picture, "Doll cake. Nan bake doll cake."

It was, indeed, a doll cake. Blessed with a creative mind and skilled in culinary arts, Shannon had transformed a plain Bundt cake into a representation of an antebellum beauty complete with hoopskirt and bonnet. To Allie, this doll cake was the loveliest confection she had ever seen, and she yearned to make one of her own. Excitedly, she tapped my arm and pointed toward the kitchen.

Sighing, I realized that our precious free time had flown by all too quickly. Over and over, I vainly tried to convince my eager daughter that I needed to get dressed for work and promised to bake a cake with her on the weekend. Her mouth set in stubborn disagreement, Allie gestured firmly toward the kitchen and resolutely pulled on me with all the strength in her stocky little body. I exhaled in relief when the pealing of the doorbell interrupted our tug of war.

Opening the front door, we greeted Jennifer, the woman who has been Allie's respite caregiver for the past eight years. Blessed with an unflappable disposition and ready smile, "Per" was a perfect match for my special little girl. She had been with us when Allie was a frail infant and had worked tirelessly to guide Allie to an upright position during toddler days. She had read hundreds of books when Allie was bedridden after surgeries, and had spent hours helping to teach Allie to talk again following a stroke and had laughed with tears in her eyes the day that Allie had triumphantly shouted her first word: "No!"

Ambling toward Jennifer with the flowered photo album clutched to her chest, Allie chattered excitedly. "Doll cake," she exhorted, "Doll cake awesome." Jennifer and I exchanged smiles at the "awesome"—Allie's favorite word, borrowed from her teenage sister. Casually explaining to Jennifer that I was hoping to fit the doll cake project into our already crowded weekend schedule, I dashed to the bedroom to change into business clothes.

Later, after six hours of nonstop telephone calls, I splashed through puddles to my van in the darkened parking lot. Driving home with windshield wipers flapping, I made a mental list of all I needed to deal with over the next few days: therapy appointments, a test to check Allie's heart function, grocery shopping, homework with Shannon, and scores of smaller tasks. Pulling into the driveway at home, I yanked up the hood of my raincoat and walked tiredly up the front steps to the house.

Before I could fit my key into the lock, Allie flung

open the door and grabbed my hand. "Doll cake, Mommy," she called out, "Allie doll cake."

Oh no, I thought in despair, *there is just no way I can deal with that doll cake tonight.* Walking reluctantly toward the kitchen, I took a deep breath as I struggled to come up with the words that would placate my excited daughter. Then, I stopped and stared in amazement at the kitchen counter.

There, centered on a large round platter, was the most beautiful doll cake in the world. Ariel the Mermaid reclined in the center of a Bundt cake glistening with waves of sea green icing. Plastic seashells adorned the base of the cake, and Flounder the Fish bobbed happily along at Ariel's side. Tears came to my eyes as my proud daughter pointed at the glorious confection and clapped her hands in glee.

"Allie bake doll cake. Per, too," she announced grandly. "Awesome doll cake."

"Awesome doll cake," I agreed. "Allie and Per made an awesome doll cake."

Pulling my chair up to the table, I watched while Allie and Jennifer cut and served their masterpiece. Relaxed and contented, I sipped a glass of milk and nibbled on the doll cake. Awesome doll cake. The most awesome doll cake in the world. Awesome Per. The most awesome caregiver in the world.

—*Sandy Keefe*

Willed

My memories of those nights I spent with my great-grandmother are still vivid. My nose tingles when I recall the scent of the Ben-Gay that she rubbed into her arthritic joints. I can see her hobbling on her bowed legs toward the bed, hear her groaning as she crawls beneath the covers, and watch her knobby fingers smoothing the blankets and tucking us in.

In my mind I hear her saying in that tone that suggested she had discovered a great secret, "Let's hold hands until we fall asleep, kid," and once again my hand is cradled within her palm. But most of all, I remember her telling me stories, kissing me gently, and whispering just before I dozed off, "Goodnight, darling."

I remember it all, because I have nothing else to remind me of her. While my friends proudly display treasures left to them by their grandmothers—

precious china, antique silver, heirloom jewelry—all that I have of Grandma's is a terrarium I'd given her that I'd made in Brownies from a baby food jar and dried flowers. All I wanted was a memento of hers that I could cherish. But Grandma's was not a china-and-jewelry kind of life.

Born February 8, 1896, in Pittsburgh, and christened Cornelia Short, she, at age twenty, married my great-grandfather and acquired the awkward appellation of Cornelia Ledergerber. We all called her Grandma Leder.

Widowed at sixty-three, she moved in with her daughter, my maternal grandmother, and devoted herself to caring for her family. During this last phase of her life was when I came to know and love her.

Grandma Leder's hair was short, gray, and frizzy from too many Toni home permanents. Earlier in life she had been heavy, but by the time I was born, her fat had melted, rendering her a five-foot, two-inch woman of the toughest gristle. Her face was round and her nose prominent, but her large, penetrating, dark brown eyes are what I remember most. With time, her hair and shape changed, but her eyes never did.

Whenever anyone was sick, needed a babysitter, or could just use an extra hand around the house, Grandma appeared on the doorstep. She was a migrant Mary Poppins, a domestic dynamo, a whirlwind of wiping, washing, and waxing.

Hard work did not intimidate Grandma; she knew nothing else. Through many nights spent with her, I learned that her father had died when she was three and that her earliest memory was of being small and standing on a chair to iron with irons so heavy she could barely lift them.

She worked all her life at menial jobs. During the Depression, she took on "confinement cases," and for a dollar a day, she moved into an expectant mother's home, kept house, cared for the children, and assisted with the baby's delivery. Well into her seventies, she helped to nurse an invalid woman.

Grandma did the dirty work. Neighbors summoned her to close the eyes and pop in the dentures of their dead. They called Grandma, because death didn't intimidate her, either—probably because she'd seen so much of it.

The saddest bedtime story she ever told me was about something that had happened to her when she was thirty-six. On a hot August day, while laughing and enjoying herself at a picnic, she heard a man calling her name on a bullhorn as he walked through the park. That man shattered the afternoon's serenity and Grandma's heart. He had been paging her so that he could take her to the morgue to identify her mother's body. While stepping off a streetcar on Pittsburgh's north side, her mother was hit by a drunk driver and thrown under a passing trolley.

Grandma never cried when she related this story. She told it straight out, evenly and slowly, and afterward, she always let out a long, deep sigh and said, "Oh, kid, it's a great life if you don't weaken." Then she squeezed my hand tightly like she was trying to hold on to me forever.

While we cuddled under the covers, she told me many other stories. I felt the anguish a mother feels when her only son is declared missing in action for a few days after D-day. I felt the sorrow a wife feels watching as throat cancer robs her beloved husband of speech and ultimately of life. I felt the despair of the Depression, what it was like to lose your home and to survive on the rotted produce that a kind-hearted neighbor scrounged for you at his market.

Grandma also told me adventure tales, how as a child she'd traveled to Steamboat Springs, Colorado, by covered wagon. And she told me funny stories. The bed shook with laughter when she recounted the time my great-grandfather polished his white shoes with zinc ointment by mistake before going to a local amusement park. We roared, picturing Grandpap strolling down the midway with all the wrappers and leaves sticking to his feet.

She told me many other stories—some of my grandmother, of my mother, and of me. The best ones she told again and again.

In 1975, when I was fifteen, she suffered a massive

stroke. After a lengthy hospital stay, my grandmother brought Grandma Leder home to die. On a hot August day, while visiting at grandmother's, my mother, who was helping to care for Grandma Leder, asked if I wanted to go in and visit with Grandma. I eagerly said yes.

But my young, innocent eyes were not prepared for the sight. I'd never looked into the face of death before. Grandma, paralyzed, had wasted to a thin layer of skin clinging to bone. I barely recognized her, except for those brown eyes. The doctors said she couldn't hear and didn't know us. But they were wrong.

In her eyes, I saw everything she ever was, and they spoke to me. Taking her hand as I had done many times when we lay together in that bed, I tried to be cheerful and positive, but I felt her eyes willing me to leave the room, begging me not to remember her this way. I left.

I never saw her alive again.

A few years ago, my life took a stressful turn, and curiously, I found Grandma and her stories frequently occupying my mind. I realized then that although Grandma had not left me any tangible keepsake, she had left me a treasury of stories and a wealth of memories. By turning her soul inside out to me during those nights in bed, she'd bequeathed me the greatest gift—her strength, her perseverance, her courage to face life head-on. Her legacy gave me the will I'd lacked. If Grandma could survive the difficulties of her life, then I knew I could, too.

Often at bedtime now, my daughter will ask that I lie with her for awhile. So, I slide beside her under the covers and whisper, "Let's hold hands until we fall asleep." Then as I hold her sweet young hand, I tell her stories. Some are Grandma Leder's, and some are mine. We sigh and giggle, and occasionally a tear falls. Then just as my child's eyelids begin to droop and her breathing becomes soft and rhythmic, I lean over and press my lips against her cool, satiny cheek. And I swear I hear a voice in the darkness whispering with me, "Goodnight, darling."

—*Janice Lane Palko*

A Bartender's Story

David frequented the small bar outside the naval shipyard most every day. The lunchtime crowd would gather around, order beers and hamburgers, and engage in lively, albeit sometimes rude, conversation. They were a motley bunch. The language was rough, and their appearances followed suit. David was among the most vocal and often the most obnoxious of the group.

The bartenders hated to see him come. At least the other guys were pleasant and polite to the bartenders and waitresses. Not David. He had a way about him that irked the girls behind the bar to their very cores.

"He thinks he's so much better than the rest of them," they often remarked.

"See how he dresses?" one said. "He even dresses better than the others to show that he has a higher position at the shipyard."

It was true. David's arrogance had won him few friends. No one knew much about him aside from his job and his lunchtime whereabouts. Most of the other guys had been in and out of the bar for years. The girls working there knew their wives' names, their kids' names, and the latest gossip in their lives. But not David's. No one knew much about him at all.

Another standout "regular" at the pub was Jeff. Homeless since his early twenties and suffering from psychotic ailments, Jeff never took his medication, preferring instead to spend his monthly Social Security check on booze. He slept under an old railroad bridge not too far from the bar.

When times got tough—typically just days before his next check would arrive at his mother's home— Jeff would often wander into the bar and ask for something to eat. This wasn't all that unusual. The homeless and the transients who were down on their luck often found their way to the bar, where they knew the waitresses would offer them a plate of eggs and toast or a bowl of soup and some bread.

Jeff, however, posed an additional problem. His hygiene was poor. It was downright disgusting. His hair was filthy and matted and most certainly infested with lice. He smelled. He was not the sort of person that paying customers would want to observe as they had their drinks or their meals.

"Come on back here, Jeff," Jeanne, the head bartender usually said, leading him to a small table off to one side of the bar. This is where the help sat to have their coffee or count up their day's tips. Out of view of most of the customers, it was the best place the girls could find to seat Jeff when he came in cold and hungry.

"Thank you, Jeanne," he always answered, his voice feeble and childlike.

Jeff kept his head down as he ate, seldom making eye contact with any of the patrons. When he left, one of the girls would thoroughly disinfect the table and chair where he'd had his meal. The dishes would immediately be run through the dishwasher on the special sanitation cycle.

One chilly March day, the head bartender saw Jeff coming, ambling down the sidewalk toward the bar. It was a particularly slow day—a perfect day to serve Jeff a meal without disturbing the customers. There was just one problem. The only patron seated at the bar that day was David.

Jeanne rolled her eyes, knowing that David would undoubtedly make rude comments about Jeff. She hoped and prayed that he wouldn't make these comments to Jeff. She filled David's mug with beer, then headed to the kitchen to place an order for Jeff.

"Jeff's coming, Mary," she told the cook. "Have you got any soup left?"

Mary nodded and busied herself preparing a large bowl of hot soup, some rolls, and a small salad.

When Jeff wandered into the bar, Jeanne noticed he was limping.

"What did you do to your foot, Jeff?" she asked.

"I don't know," he answered. "It hurts."

Jeanne led him to the usual table and brought his food. She kept a nervous eye on David and hoped that by filling his mug she'd keep him quiet.

Her hopes were shattered just a minute into Jeff's meal.

"Hi, young fella," David greeted Jeff.

Jeanne sucked in her breath, ready to take a shot at the man who would most certainly insult this unfortunate.

"Mind if I join you?" David asked him.

"No," Jeff answered softly.

"What happened to your foot?" he asked.

"I dunno. It's both feet. They hurt," Jeff answered.

"How long has it been since you've had a bath or a shower?" David asked him.

Oh, no. Jeanne stood perched like a cat ready to pounce, ready for that good-for-nothing David to say something to insult Jeff. *David had probably never gone without a meal or a hot shower one day in his life. How dare he suggest that this poor homeless man was any less of a human being because he had?*

"Jeanne, I'll be right back," David said, laying a ten-dollar bill on the bar next to his mug.

"Don't hurry," she muttered under her breath, as she took a fresh pot of coffee to Jeff's table.

David wasn't gone fifteen minutes. Returning to the bar, Jeanne noticed he carried a paper bag from the store a few doors down.

"Fill 'er up, Jeanne," he said, nodding toward his mug on the bar. "And keep your customers down at that end when they come in."

The nerve! Who did this guy think he was? He couldn't tell her where to seat her customers!

What she observed next, however, floored her.

David went to the kitchen and asked Mary for a large pot. Taking it to the restroom, he emerged with it filled with hot soapy water. Pulling his items from the bag, he then set a bar of soap, a washcloth, some ointment, bandages, and clean socks on Jeff's table.

"Let's get those old boots off," he said to Jeff. He spoke in the sweetest, most gentle voice Jeanne had ever heard him use.

Jeff complied.

David crumpled up the filthy socks—riddled with holes—and stuffed them into the bag from the store.

Tears formed in Jeanne's eyes as she watched what happened next.

Delicately, David took one of Jeff's feet in his

hands. He dipped the washcloth in the pot of water, lathered it with the fresh bar of soap, and began to tenderly wash Jeff's foot. Patting it dry with paper towels from the restroom, he proceeded to wash Jeff's other foot in the same manner.

When both feet were clean and dry, David applied ointment and bandages to the swollen, open sores. He then slipped the soft, clean white socks over Jeff's newly washed and mended feet.

"There," he said to Jeff. "That should feel much better."

"It does," Jeff said humbly. "Thank you."

"You're welcome."

Word spread quickly of what David had done for Jeff. Other employees and bar patrons wondered if Jeanne was making up the story, but when they saw her change in attitude toward the surly customer, they knew she told the truth.

Within weeks they knew more about David. He was divorced. He had a son he saw every few weeks and an ex-wife with whom he'd developed a decent friendship. He lived in a rooming house during the week while he worked at the shipyard.

In his hometown he was a deacon in his church. This struck the girls at the bar as odd; they fully expected a church deacon to wear a stuffy suit and tie and to carry a Bible.

Far more than Jeff's feet were transformed on

that chilly March day. The hearts of several hardened bartenders and waitresses also began softening, too. After that day they didn't judge quite so quickly and so harshly. For in David, they had discovered Christlike qualities in someone they had judged to be arrogant and callous, and not a disciple of compassion. They watched him minister to the poor and the sick. They saw all this while they filled his mug with beer and served free hot meals to the least among them.

—*Kimberly Ripley*

The Wonder of Now

*I*n the photograph, my sixteen-year-old son is standing
on the deck of a bright yellow boat called the Beast.
*The wind is blowing his hair into exuberant disarray. The
World Trade Center towers and the buildings of lower
Manhattan loom in the background. My son is in profile,
half facing the camera, half facing the Twin Towers—as
if he is unable to completely break from the city's pull. His
half-exposed smile matches his hair, an unaffected expression of joyous anticipation. The sky is vivid blue. At the
bottom of the photo is written:*

New York, June, 2001

In my closet I have boxes of photographs. These
are the ones that have never made it to positions of
honor in frames, in albums, or on the refrigerator door.

The New York photograph was immediately put
on the refrigerator. Originally, it was put up for one

reason; it stayed there for another. But thinking about it, the reasons were just variations of the same theme, made more dramatic by the turn of events. But that is getting ahead of the story.

First, you must understand the trip. And to understand the trip, you must first understand the promise.

I'm not sure when the promise was made. It could have been on one of the traditional dates I used to take with each of my children to mark summer's end.

"When you are sixteen, we will go to New York," I might have said.

It could have happened that way, but I am not certain. But I do know that it became a given that, when a child turned sixteen, the "date" would be in New York City.

I also know that the promise was made long before the substance of our lives changed—before their father moved us to San Francisco, then to Chicago, then left the family and took a new wife. Certainly long before that.

That, however, changed everything about the promise. The promise was light and dreamy, and life became dark and practical. But darkness is a funny thing. If you're in it long enough, you can more easily spot what's important.

So when Matthew, the oldest, turned sixteen, I gave him a tour guide book to Manhattan.

"We're going?" he asked.

"We're going," I said.

Now, there are fears intrinsically involved with any vacation, fueled by change of routine and apprehension of the unknown, but this one carried extra baggage. I needed New York to come through big— bigger than uneventful taxi and subway rides, adequate accommodations, and follow-throughs on plays and concerts. I needed a New York jolt to the senses—when the noise and crowds and colors and aromas transform ordinary streets into brilliant displays of surprise, interest, and possibilities.

To be honest, I needed it as much as my son did. For a year, grief had colored our world in monochromatic drabness. There was an inability to appreciate the present—which seemed to have become, more and more, just an unattractive stepchild to the past.

The day we took the ride on the *Beast*, we had walked down to lower Manhattan to meet one of my friends for lunch. We then went to Wall Street and finally made our way past the Towers. We watched the people for awhile. They seemed busy and confident and purposeful.

When we finally got to the boat and I snapped that carefree, disheveled picture of Matt, it marked both an end and the beginning.

Maybe I would have been the only one to see the difference in his eyes, maybe not. But the trip had worked its magic, and something had happened to both of us. The picture became my proof—a capture of a "gee, isn't life wonderful and interesting and I can't wait to get on with it" look.

My only regret was that Matt wasn't faced fully forward, so I could see his face completely.

That was the first reason the picture went up on the refrigerator, this victorious return of wonder.

And the picture stayed up after the skyline changed—even though, after that happened, I avoided looking at it. And when I did, I saw only the Towers, which suddenly seemed to cast mocking shadows on Matt's happy smile.

But I never took the picture down.

Matt and I returned to New York to visit a college in October 2002, going back to the hotel where we had stayed on our original visit. One late afternoon, Matt decided to go to Times Square, and I opted to take a small walk on our quiet street.

Shortly into the walk I noticed a small park that had not been there on our previous visit. I crossed the street to sit down on a small bench. It was almost sundown on a very gray day.

In the center of the park was a small monument. I walked over to look at it.

On the monument were names of firefighters from the area who had died. "September 11, 2001," it read. There were probably a dozen of them.

I touched the names.

Then I went back to the park bench. There was an unusual quietness to this street, but up the block I could see the busyness of Broadway. People moving purposefully up the street. Taxis rushing. Horns blowing. Melodic music from street performers. Laughter. Shouting.

The whole messy mix of life.

I could see the colors, not the faces. They stood in contrast to the grayness and became, I thought, a busy human rainbow.

I stayed for a while, and then went back to the room.

When we returned home, the photograph had taken on a new meaning.

The Towers no longer seemed to be looming tragic symbols, coloring everything in shadows. They became, rather, angelic reminders of our responsibilities to tend to the wonders of now.

The minutes. The smiles. The wind. The sky. The colors. The shouting. The laughter. The streets teeming in difference. All of the possibilities we have, just because we are here.

My son's transfixed half turn of the head now seemed perfectly appropriate. Life, with all of its fragile wonders, should always be pulling us in.

And so the picture remains.

—Sue Vitou

Practical Magic

The people in the corridor didn't know. How could they? Nurses, doctors, orderlies, interns, patients, visitors—all in a hurry to get some-place else.

While some hurried from Point A to Point B, others moved in slow, measured steps, their grip on the handrail making their knuckles white. Glancing into the nondescript room as they passed by, these various people would have seen a gray-haired patient, a grandfatherly sort, in his sixties. They might have noted the young woman sitting near the bed, raven-haired and pretty, about the right age to be his granddaughter.

None would witness the miracle taking place within those drab walls. It was subtle and easy to overlook, easily mistaken for a typical visit between patient and visitor, most certainly a loved one. But it was no typical visit. It was magic. Of the most potent, all-too-uncommon sort, far too grand to notice in a passing glance.

As the moments blinked by, the frail man painted his lifetime—his words were his brush strokes. That was only half of the magic.

The real magic was that she listened. And heard.

The clock on his life was winding down. He struggled to walk across the room. But his words still had power. So it was with words that he whisked his visitor off to times long past and places half a world away. Times and places he hadn't been able to take anyone to for a long time.

His family didn't mean to keep him in a box, unseen, unheard. They were just too busy—or too preoccupied with his illness—to take a station break and meander through the past with him again. They already knew his stories forward and backward. They didn't understand that he had to share his memories, that in sharing he could relive them, feel alive again.

As the young woman sat in the sturdy, no-frills hospital chair and listened, the old man stood in the footprints of a lanky high school boy, ashamed he hadn't set one foot outside the borders of Oregon. On his eighteenth birthday, with only the mighty Columbia River between him and Washington, he dove in. He swam hard enough to reach another state. And then, after collapsing on the far shore with his chest heaving from the effort, he swam back.

He rooted about in his memories and found every treasured arrowhead over again, and relived the rescue of a long list of injured animals. As the minutes passed, he grew into the tender recruit who served his country in World War II. On the day two of his buddies were drafted into the Army, he decided he wanted to choose his own destiny and join the Navy. The only obstacle was the sixty miles between him and the recruiting station.

It was a bitterly cold winter day. He set his face for Portland, climbed aboard his bike with the big, fat tires, and started to pedal. He rode all night. The hairs inside his nose froze. He stopped in a Portland diner, counted his change, and ordered a steaming bowl of chili to thaw himself out. It was what he could afford. And then, he enlisted.

His Navy stories were rich and vivid, full of Australia, a country he learned to love. His visitor saw him at his best, the way he was before the world wore him down.

Of course, he saved his most precious story for last.

He stepped back into a day in Norfolk, Virginia. . . .

Walking along Gramby Street, he was making his way back to the submarine to ship out. Then, she walked by. It was a busy, crowded sidewalk, but he spotted her instantly—and she took his breath away. He didn't know her, didn't even get to meet her, but somehow she made his heart ache.

His heart ached for the lovely stranger for another decade. . . .

Until the night he met the same woman face-to-face at a dance in Alaska, half a world away. He decided that very night to marry her, and told his best friend so. Only six weeks later, they said "I do."

Still, the young woman beside the hospital bed listened.

And the magic grew stronger.

Because she listened, he was transformed. Because she was interested, he managed to leave behind the tubes and monitors and pain. Because she heard what he had to tell, he was able to make a journey of his own.

He stepped out across time, and for a few moments, he could feel the cloth of a younger man's shirt on his back, the arms of a young soldier holding his bride.

He received a great gift that day, one his closest family members hadn't thought to give—the chance to relive his life simply in its telling. But he was not the only one to be so gifted that day, for the listener cherished his retelling of a life well lived—a treasure his closest family members had missed.

He died soon after that special visit. But in the chilly twilight hours of his life, he'd had more than hospital linens to keep him warm. On a day that seemed quite ordinary, he'd found the strength to share himself one more time. And his raven-haired visitor breathed life into his memories by listening.

The man in the hospital room was my father. I wish I had been the wise young woman in the chair.

—Christy Caballero

Incidental Kin

Whenever he bleeds now, it is my blood he sheds. On mornings when I am especially rushed, I often mishandle the razor while shaving my legs in the shower. While the water rinses the wound, I imagine that he might be shaving his face, untold miles away. Perhaps he, too, has inadvertently nicked himself; the blood coloring the tissue he uses to stanch the flow is the same blood that streams down my shower drain. Even the most expert pathologist could not detect a difference, because no difference exists.

He bleeds my blood because of simple chance, the exquisitely random circumstance of gene variety and selection. He needed a bone marrow transplant, and I, a stranger to him, proved a perfect match.

I am curious about him, but rules made to ensure privacy and for the protection of both parties prevent me from knowing anything other than his gender (male) and his age group (young adult). The odds that he would find a suitable blood match were one in 20,000. I ask myself: *What are the odds that I might find him revolting? What if we differ in political views or moral philosophies? What plans does he have for the rest of his life? What, I wonder, has he cherished, vowed, hoped, forgiven?*

Because he could be anyone, he becomes, instead, the nameless, faceless everyone.

One month before the scheduled donation date, I went to the transplant center to give additional blood and urine samples to confirm my physical well-being. As I returned to my car, two little girls, perhaps three and four years old, exited the elevators of the parking garage, followed by a man of indeterminate age. Although taller than I, he appeared to weigh much less, and he carried his wasted frame carefully. He slowly made his way to his truck and with obvious effort, boosted both girls, slight as flowers, into it.

I sat in my car, watching him, wondering if he could be the one who would receive my marrow. I knew the odds were against it: On any given day, 3,000 potential recipients wait for a donor.

Soon afterward, I learned that my recipient had commenced chemotherapy to destroy his own marrow and make room for mine and to suppress his immune system so it would be optimally receptive to the new cells. Once this process has begun, there is no going back. Either the patient receives new marrow, or he dies.

The marrow aspiration took place on a cool fall morning two weeks past my thirtieth birthday. The hospital staff was courteous and efficient. I was given an epidural and put to sleep. The surgery lasted forty minutes; later, I learned that the doctors worried whether in the quickness of the procedure they had removed more liquid than cells. Postsurgical tests run on the marrow, however, showed a high cell count.

I woke up after the surgery a bit woozy, the second of two autologous blood units dripping into my vein. For me, the intravenous fluids represented little: hastened recovery, renewed energy. But in a place not far from where I lay, another intravenous tube transferred my marrow into the recipient's bloodstream, from which the cells would instinctively find their way into his bones. For him, these roughly two pints of spongy, red material represented nothing less than his future.

I've always considered myself to be an optimist, yet I could not fathom the tremendous amount of hope contained in those bags. No, not hope—something beyond hope. The substance in those bags was pure prayer: earnest, liquefied prayer.

The anesthesia left me nauseous for about

twenty-four hours, but I experienced no major complications. I was back to work in three days and resumed light exercise in two weeks. I impatiently awaited news of the recipient.

Once in a while someone asks me why I donated bone marrow to a person I knew nothing about. I usually reply that it's he who has done the amazing, by risking his life in order to save it and by having such faith in a complete stranger. It's an easy, stock answer, and one that seems to satisfy most. But even I know it doesn't begin to explain the reason why.

A few years ago, my father's eldest brother fell ill with cirrhosis of the liver. He immediately quit drinking, but the damage had been done. By the time he started throwing up blood, all the late-arriving assistance we could summon was just that: too late.

When I went to visit him in the facility where he was being cared for, I was shocked to find him shrunken almost beyond recognition. He gave no indication that he even knew I was there. He seemed thirsty, and I gave him some water, but his teeth chattered as if he was chilled by a coldness that ran inside-out, far beyond the reach of any earthly relief.

My uncle was dying and with him would go my father's last remaining sibling from a family of five children. Feeling both inept and irrelevant, I kept my visit short. Upon hearing of his death a few days later, I immediately regretted what I had been given the opportunity to do, but had not. I wished that I had climbed onto his bed, placed his head in my lap, and stroked his forehead until his teeth stopped chattering and he fell asleep.

This is what I wished, and I wish it now as I wished it then, without hope, in the truly forsaken manner that I will continue to wish it for the rest of my life. It is this fervent, hopeless wish, and the cold undercurrent of shame that still flows strong and black beneath it, that serve to remind me that I am not noble. On the contrary: I owe, I am in debt.

Three weeks after my aspiration, I receive word that the recipient is doing well and the marrow is engrafting onto his bones. The impossible has happened: Someone whom I've never met shares my personal—yet no longer individual—genetic typing and is closer to me, in some respects, than a blood relative. I think of the person whose veins now carry my blood and of the 3,000 others who today need a donor. Some of them will not last the day, having run out of time. May a kind hand stay and soothe them to sleep.

—Brenda Fritsvold

 # Sweet Moments

I was not enjoying my life. Too many big things were changing for the worse, and the good things that trickled in were almost too trivial to notice.

"What am I doing wrong?" I asked aloud one morning, while looking at myself in the mirror.

I wanted a sign from the universe, some event or symbol to guide me in the right direction. I had received such symbols before—an unexpected project when I was stewing over money, a phone call from an old friend I've been thinking about for weeks, another friend leaving me a gift of homemade banana bread for no reason at all.

But though I searched my daily life for clues and signs, though I prayed for guidance and even occasionally meditated, I neither saw, found, nor felt any stirrings of divine guidance.

Unless you count donuts.

The morning I began my quest, I got into my car, turned on my audiobook, and listened to a scene in which two men are eating donuts in a small-town diner. I hadn't eaten a donut in years and could just barely imagine the sweet taste. The story moved on to murder, beautiful manipulative women, and threatened thoroughbred horses. Despite the intricate plot, all I could think about was that glazed donut.

The next day, I opened a magazine to an article about the best pastries in the United States. In among the French pastries, flaky pies, and rich tortes lounged a chocolate-covered donut.

I stepped out of my car at the grocery store and nearly stepped on half a smashed jelly donut right beside my tire.

I turned on National Public Radio and heard that Krispy Kreme donuts had strong quarterly earnings.

I opened a local newspaper and learned that an area donut shop had become kosher.

I started to think, maybe my life decisions were somehow intertwined with sweet circles of fried dough. After all, I knew that prayers were often answered in unusual ways, from burning bushes to manna falling from the sky.

But what meaning could a donut possibly have? I stared at the picture of the newspaper's food section and considered its potential for mystical properties:

~ A holey center
~ A powerful sweetness
~ Well rounded

Or maybe the donut was trying to tell me to just buckle down and earn more dough!

I folded up the newspaper and flipped on the television to watch the news. A donut commercial appeared.

It was time to take action.

The next morning, I dropped into a donut shop and ordered one glazed. As I waited, I watched the conveyor belt jostle hundreds of donuts along an intricate and slightly old-fashioned-looking system. They rose on a narrow pulley through a baking chamber, then spread on a conveyor belt and got drenched with a shower of sugary glaze. They continued until they were boxed and served, still warm from their journey.

"How many donuts do you make every day?" I asked the clerk, as he rang up my glazed and coffee.

"About sixty thousand," he told me and smiled as my mouth dropped open.

I sat down to experience my treat. My first bite was delicious. My second bite was heavenly. *Eat slowly,* I advised myself, but I couldn't. I loved the way the hunk of sweet dough melted away in my mouth and the little spangles of glaze fell onto my plate.

As I ate, a girl with a ponytail and cell phone came in and interrupted her conversation to buy two dozen assorted. A man parked a silver-plated meat delivery truck outside and ran in to get a cheesecake donut, a chocolate cake donut, and a large coffee. Cars moved steadily through the drive-through, and big boxes containing dozens flowed from clerk to window.

A thin, shaky gentleman had to push hard to get the door open. He rested against the counter, catching his breath, before ordering a glazed with sprinkles. He fumbled in his pocket and spilled fifty cents across the counter.

"It's sixty-four cents, sir," the clerk told him.

The man leaned one hand on the glass case and spidered the other hand into one pants pocket, then the other, then the pockets in his ancient beige windbreaker. A blue ink pen and a wadded tissue emerged.

"I have change," I said, getting up and handing over a quarter.

"It's here somewhere," the man said, his voice like paper in wind. "Thank you, though, thank you. I have no business eating this donut, but I seem to want it."

I smiled. I could say the same thing about myself. I held the door open for the man and sat back down to savor my last bites.

All too soon, I had eaten my donut. I wanted another one, but hurriedly left before I could indulge.

In the parking lot, I passed the thin man, sitting in a large white-and-black Buick, polishing off his donut.

I smiled, feeling good that I had contributed a little something to another person's happiness. I smiled even more when I found a nickel on the asphalt outside my car door.

Was this the answer to my prayers: to simply add small sweetnesses to other people's lives and to my own?

I had one flake of glaze on my index finger, which I carefully licked off and savored before I got into my car and drove to work.

—*Deborah H. Shouse*

One Man and a Whole Lot of Somebodies

At the age of sixteen, Chuck Ambler went to work for a small drugstore chain. He took a job as a stock-boy after school. While his friends were playing football and basketball, Chuck was stocking shelves. Chuck's father was a volunteer firefighter, and on one life-altering evening, he did not return home. Chuck's father had died at the age of fifty-three.

Over the next thirty-three years, the company, Rite-Aid Pharmacy, grew into one of the largest drugstore chains in the United States. Chuck grew along with it. He advanced from stock-boy to regional vice president, after doing almost every job involved in running a retail operation. Chuck buffed the floors, worked the cash registers, cleaned the restrooms, and took out the trash.

Chuck now runs a major East Coast region of the

chain, which now consists of more than 200 stores and a few thousand employees. When Chuck enters a store, he makes a point of greeting every employee by name. A hardworking and devoted manager, he leads by example and has earned the respect and loyalty of all his staff.

One day Chuck asked me to help him write a letter to company headquarters. Chuck and I had worked together many years earlier, but I'd since left the company and Chuck was now my husband. I informed him that I had no idea how to write a professional business letter; after all, I was not a secretary. He explained that he didn't want a professional letter. He wanted me to tell Donna's story, and he would take it from there. Not a problem, I told him, since I had remained friends with Donna after I'd left the company.

Donna and I had shared many slices of pizza and tears over the years. Our favorite pastime was a childlike game of "who's worse." She always insisted it was me, and I let her know she was out of her mind. I have multiple sclerosis; Donna has cancer. We always agreed to disagree and clinked together our mugs of beer in a toast to us, two disease-ridden women in our thirties, hanging onto life with all our might and one another's friendship. Orange grease would drizzle down our chins as we devoured our pizza. On these days, we couldn't have cared less about calories or fat grams. These were medically necessary mental health lunches. Donna had issues that were more pressing than if her jeans would fit tomorrow. My job was to make her laugh as best I could and to listen, often as Donna bargained with God.

"I just want to see Kendall graduate from eighth grade," she would choke out. "Is that too much to ask, Beth?"

The cancer had first appeared five years earlier. Donna had been gazing out the window watching her eight-year-old daughter, Kendall, playing. Smiling at the joyous sight, she had absentmindedly reached under her armpit and scratched an itch. She felt a hard pea-size lump, and her stomach did a belly flop. There was a time when Donna would have ignored it, but now she was a mother and things were different.

Many doctor visits and tests confirmed she had breast cancer. Donna was thirty-eight when she lost her breast. A few weeks later, she was well enough to return to work. Over the next five years, the cancer would continue to return, randomly attacking different parts of her body. First, the tumors moved to her legs. She underwent more chemotherapy and grueling treatment. This time, she lost all her hair and wore a beret when she returned to work. Over pizza, we agreed she looked a little funny with no eyelashes, but not having to shave her legs was a bonus. And then we raised our beers together in our traditional toast.

The tumors spread rapidly throughout Donna's legs and hips, and she was in a great deal of pain. She was hospitalized again, that time to insert steel rods into her legs, for fear her bones would shatter.

At the time, Donna was a store manager and had worked for the company for twenty years. She had run out of sick days and vacation time. Her first bout with cancer had also used up the state short-term disability pay. She had no choice but to go back to work once she'd healed from the leg surgery. She needed her paycheck. Cancer wreaked havoc on both her body and her bank account. Copays add up when your medical bills are in the tens of thousands.

She was still not cancer-free when she returned to work. Donna was tough, but her resolve was weakening. Always in pain and exhausted, she would suck down Advil tablets as if they were M&Ms and go to work. The doctor had given her a prescription for Oxycoton, a very strong pain medication commonly prescribed for cancer, but she would have been unable to do her job while under the influence of such a strong painkiller.

That was what had prompted Chuck to write the letter. On a scheduled visit to Donna's store that day, he had seen that she was weak and in excruciating pain. He was the one who had hired Donna twenty years earlier, and it broke his heart to see her in such agony.

"She is going to die if we don't get her home to heal and fight the cancer. She can't keep working." Chuck sighed.

"Somebody's got to do something! Can't the company make an exception and just pay her?" I cried.

"We have gotten too big for that. It wouldn't be legal. But trust me, Beth, I am working on a solution. Just write the letter for me, as Donna's friend."

And so I did. I poured out my heart to a large, faceless corporation. I pleaded with them to help, to please do something. I appealed to them on behalf of Donna's eight-year-old daughter. I told them they could do nothing, of course, and just let her die. I'd learned from my mother how to use guilt; I had no shame. I begged and reasoned and cajoled and dared them to step up to the plate for their seriously ill twenty-year employee. I gave the letter to Chuck.

The next week Chuck spoke with the corporate office. He asked the legal department and human resource office to review his plan. They agreed, confirmed that the plan was legal, and he got the approval he needed.

Chuck e-mailed a revised copy of the letter to all of the managers in his region. He named the program the Send Donna Home Campaign.

To respect her privacy, he did not use her full

name. Chuck told them that one of their fellow managers had cancer, and she needed to take a leave of absence to get well—and to get paid while she was home. His goal was to raise the payroll dollars needed to pay Donna's salary during her absence with vacation time donated from each of them. It was purely volunteer and anonymous. They could donate as little as one hour's vacation pay, if they chose. He needed 1,800 vacation payroll hours.

Word spread quickly. Some figured out who Donna was, but many did not. Hundreds of e-mails started pouring in, jamming Chuck's computer. Managers sent their love and hope to the unknown woman. Payroll dollars were donated faster than Chuck could have imagined. Some managers were donating full weeks of their hard-earned vacation time. Cashiers were giving up two to three days' pay. And every donor sent a personal note to the Donna with cancer. Most of them wrote that if more payroll vacation dollars were needed, they would gladly give more. Many said they would start a prayer vigil in their churches, their temples, their mosques, all for Donna.

Within the week, the news had spread to the New York region. They, too, wanted to help. Chuck thanked them, but told them it wouldn't be necessary. By the end of the next week, Chuck's goal of raising one year's worth of payroll hours had doubled. The employees in Chuck's region had donated enough time to send Donna home for two years with pay and full medical benefits.

Donna and Chuck met for lunch that week. He wanted to give her the news in person. She was stunned at first, and then the tears started to flow. He showed her the e-mails from people she didn't even know. She could not believe that so many people would help her and that her boss would do something so incredible for her. She wondered aloud how she would ever be able to thank Chuck and all those amazing people. Suddenly, a corporation was not a nameless, faceless entity; it was a community of caring people, each with a face, a heart, a name, and a little bit of time and love to share.

Chuck smiled and said, "Somebody had to do something. You need to see your daughter grow up. I need you to get well and run the best darn pharmacy the chain has. You get well and show up for work. That is how you will thank all these somebodies."

During the two-year period that Donna was at home, the cancer spread to her brain. She called me the day she got the news.

"I won." She said into the phone. I was confused for a second.

"I have a brain tumor. I just won the Who Is Worse contest."

I was speechless.

"Are you there, Beth?"

I regained my composure and continued the conversation as best as I could.

Donna was right. She is the winner. In the next two years, she had brain surgery, radiation treatment, and chemotherapy. Last year, the cancer went into remission, and her doctors feel confident that Donna might have won the war.

Chuck's eyes filled with tears when I told him that Donna is in remission. Donna has since returned to work as a manager of one of Chuck's stores.

On Donna's first day back to work, Chuck sent everyone in his region an e-mail announcing her return to health and to work, and again thanking them for their contributions. Once again, the responding e-mails clogged his computer, as hundreds of people expressed how blessed they felt in helping Donna and thanking Chuck for the opportunity.

Today, Donna is feeling great and is still cancer-free and hard at work. I told my husband, Chuck, how proud I am of him, and that I am sure his father would have been, too. He was the somebody who stepped forward and did something, and who prompted a whole lot of other somebodies to do something, too.

—*Beth Rothstein Ambler*

Over the Hill

"You are unemployable," the young woman said, reaching across her desk to return my resume.

Stunned, I stared at her. The expression on her face seemed smug, reflecting security in her own position. She rose, terminating my interview.

Getting shakily to my feet, I ducked my head to hide hot tears threatening to spill. I crammed my carefully prepared resume into my purse. With what dignity I could muster, I mumbled "Thanks," turned, and hurried out of the employment agency.

Climbing unsteadily into my car, I leaned my head on the steering wheel and let the tears flow. *Help me, God,* I prayed.

At forty-four years old, recently divorced, unexpectedly alone with teenage children and myself to support, out of the job market for eighteen years, I had four months of job hunting behind me.

At first, I had not worried. Although lacking a college degree (I had married and left university my junior year), I was widely read. I had been a secretary before the children came. Though I typed with only four fingers in my own hit-and-hope method, I was accurate and fast. My shorthand was minimal, but in most offices, it was no longer needed. Word processors were, by then, common, and I felt confident I could learn to use one. But I needed a job now to put food on the table, and I could not wait for extensive training. Given a chance, I felt sure that I could be of use somewhere. But those words, "You are unemployable," rang in my ears and frightened me to the core.

It was a hot summer afternoon. Reluctant to go home and tell my children of this latest failed interview, I drove down Main Street and back, and parked in the only shady space. I slumped down in my seat.

I had called on the major companies in town. I had answered newspaper advertisements. I had asked everyone I knew to tell me of any openings they learned of. Health problems ruled out factory work. My only experience, years before, was in office work.

In more than thirty interviews, I had been told I was unqualified and "over the hill," despite recent laws forbidding age discrimination. Trying a high-fee employment agency seemed the last option. Yet, even there, the youthful counselor had refused to accept my application and resume.

Unemployable, she had said. What if I was? What if I couldn't find a job before my money ran out? What would happen to us? Please, God, show me what to do, I pleaded silently.

It was almost five o'clock. Shops were closing. Blotting my tears, I saw that I was parked in front of a shabby building. A sign over a small door between two stores read "Temp Services."

In near desperation I left the car and walked toward the sign. Following a faded arrow, I stepped inside and climbed steep stairs.

I half expected the temporary employment service to be closed. Instead an "open" sign was tacked on the door. I walked into a plainly furnished office. A dark-haired woman about my age sat at an old wooden desk. Without interrupting her telephone conversation, she waved me toward a lumpy-cushioned couch. A bulletin board behind her held job listings for day labor and factory work.

When she finished her call, the woman smiled and said, "I always have a cup of tea before I close up. Would you like one?"

"Yes, please," I answered.

I watched as she dropped tea bags into chipped mugs and added water from an electric kettle. She brought me a mug, sat down beside me, and put her feet up on the low table in front of us.

"I don't know why, but hot tea makes me feel better, even in summer. My name is Mary. How can I help you?" she asked.

Suddenly, words tumbled out. I told Mary my story from the day I got divorced and we moved to this southern town to start a new life, to my shock when the employment counselor had pronounced me "unemployable."

I heard my voice grow shrill. Yet, Mary listened quietly. Then she asked about my life as wife, mother, homemaker. She was sympathetic. She asked if I had done volunteer work. I fished out my crumpled resume and handed it to her. As we sipped our tea, she read it.

"May I keep this?" she asked at last.

"Of course."

"What do you think you could do best in an office?" she inquired.

"I'm told I write great letters. I'm good at organizing. I learn fast," I told her.

Minutes passed. She finished her tea. Then she looked me squarely in the eyes and said, "My dear, you have the most important qualifications an employer looks for. You're honest, you need work, and you will show up every day to put in a full day's work. You know how to juggle several tasks at once. It takes a good coordinator to manage a family and home. There is a place for you, and we'll find it."

Could this be true? Mary believed in me. She did not see me as over the hill and unemployable.

She rose, and I followed. She told me not to worry. She gave me a typing test, which I passed. With an encouraging hand on my arm, she walked me to the door and added, "I promise I'll call you soon."

With renewed hope in my heart, I nearly ran down the stairs and hurried home.

Two days passed. Then another. My confidence waned. Would Mary truly call as she had promised?

Each time the telephone rang, I jumped. I was afraid to leave the house in case I might miss Mary's call. Nearly a week later, I sat watching the telephone, willing it to ring. At last it did.

"Hello!" Mary's voice was cheery. "A man has called who needs you for two weeks. He's starting a fishing tackle company and wants someone who writes good letters and can work unsupervised. If you get along, this could become permanent. Can you start tomorrow morning at eight?"

Could I!

"I know nothing about fishing," I warned her.

"Doesn't matter. This gentleman wants an honest worker who is mature and can be left on her own a lot," Mary said. "It's perfect for you."

"Mary, you don't know what this means." I blurted out along with my thanks.

The pay for two weeks would be meager, but it was a beginning. A chance.

After Mary rang off, I sat staring at the telephone, thinking back over the week. If I had not felt so devastated by the first interviewer that fateful day, I would not have lingered downtown. Or parked in that one space along Main Street that was a haven of shade and found a haven of another sort. Coincidence? I think not.

On the brink of despair, I had reluctantly climbed those worn stairs and found a compassionate woman of vision who had said, "There is a place for you, and we'll find it."

A prayer answered. A promise made and kept. So began the first step in a positive direction . . . over the hill . . . where my future was very bright, indeed.

—*Marcia E. Brown*

For the Love of Pixie

I was in my junior year in high school when I started dating Brian McCloud. He came from a large family, and had an older brother and three younger sisters. His father was a large, rugged man who never really talked; he bellowed out orders. Brian's mother—nicknamed Pixie, because she was so tiny—was a patient but feisty woman who, when she'd had enough of the noise, would stop it with one look. It was very obvious that Brian's parents adored one another; they just had a funny way of showing it.

A terrible thing happened during my first summer with the McClouds. Brian's mother was backing down the driveway in her car when she saw their newspaper on the ground. She stopped the car, opened the door, and as she leaned out to try to pick up the paper, her foot slipped and hit the gas pedal. The car lurched backward, and her head smashed into a telephone pole.

Karen, the youngest daughter, was in the car with her mother, and she started screaming at the top of her lungs. It was a horrible sight for her to see. Brian's father rushed out of the house and found the comatose body of his wife in their driveway. The car had backed across the street and onto the sidewalk. He ran over, yanked Karen out of the car, and ran into the house to call 911. An ambulance rushed Pixie to the hospital. The trauma to her head had caused her to have a stroke. She was in a coma for several weeks.

Her recovery took quite some time. Her right side was paralyzed, and she had difficulty speaking. After undergoing extensive physical and speech therapy, she was eventually allowed to return home. To me, she seemed to be the same, only a little quieter and weaker. Everyone was happy to have her back, especially in the kitchen; Pixie was a wonderful cook.

Her stay at home was, unfortunately, short-lived. One morning she suffered a massive stroke and was unconscious until Brian's brother, Tim, found her. She suffered two additional strokes while in the hospital. She lost all motor control, could not speak, and was placed in a wheelchair. The doctors told Brian's father that her condition would not improve and that she would slowly deteriorate. They recommended she be placed in a rest home. Brian's father refused, and against the advice of the medical professionals, he brought Pixie home.

Pixie was basically in a degenerative state and could do nothing for herself. Brian's father was absolutely sure that Pixie had some cognitive abilities and mandated that all of us, me included, learn how to care for her. Not only would we bathe her, dress her, feed her, and take her to the bathroom, we would also behave. Swearing, arguing, fighting, and other inappropriate behavior were forbidden. Brian's father was determined that Pixie's life would be as good as possible. He felt certain that she could hear everything and that her mind still functioned.

I've never seen a family come together the way the McClouds did when Pixie came home. Five children ranging in age from ten to seventeen years old took to heart their roles in supporting their father's wishes. Not only did they assume full responsibility for cleaning the house and learning how to cook, they also began to care for the mother who had held them in her arms and devoted her life to her children and husband. I helped Brian bathe his mother and watched as he gently talked to her while washing and rinsing her hair. I helped Karen with the cooking and cleaning as much as I could. Elizabeth, the oldest daughter, spent the most time with her mother and loved to read to her. I was fascinated with the way they all included their mother in conversations, even though she never spoke or acknowledged their presence.

The way Brian's father took care of Pixie touched my heart most of all. After a hard day of working construction, he would come home, get cleaned up, and go straight to wherever Pixie was. He'd pick her up and carry her over to the large rocking chair in the living room. There he would sit, rocking her and whispering into her ear. He told her over and over how beautiful she was and how much he loved her. Watching this big burly man, who could make the bravest person cower when he yelled, hold Pixie gently in his arms like she was a small child always touched me deeply. Witnessing him dealing day by day with the loss of the person his wife had once been, I realized how much courage, resolve, and devotion it must have taken for him to hold onto whatever was left and to bring the family together to do it.

About a year later, Pixie died. She passed on peacefully in her sleep. Although the woman they'd known had been gone for a long time, when Pixie died, the family was heartbroken. After high school, I stopped seeing Brian and eventually moved on with my own life. But I have never forgotten the McClouds. I will always remember and admire their unity, strength, and devotion during a very difficult time.

—*Leigh P. Rogers*

The Picture on the Wall

When I go to my friend Sue Ann's house, the first thing I see is a picture on the wall. It is neither a Van Gogh nor a Salvador Dali, neither pretty nor artistic. It is a crayon drawing of a house with stick children playing in the front yard, hung on the wall in a simple frame. This picture is special to Sue Ann, which is why it holds a special place in her home.

Sue Ann used to live in a duplex, where she also ran a small day care center that my children attended. The house was in disrepair, and the owner-landlord routinely refused to make the repairs. For that and other reasons, Sue Ann longed to own her own house. Homeownership not only offered comfort, security, and stability, it would also provide visual evidence that she had beaten the statistics and stereotype of the single mother. As a divorcée with three children whose father paid no child support, she had worked hard to save money for a down payment and had managed to slowly put away a substantial sum. Unfortunately, because she owned her own business and due to financial debt accrued during her marriage, the bank required a larger down payment and, consequently, turned down her mortgage application. Sue Ann had hoped to purchase a house and move during the summer of 2001. By fall, her savings still fell far short of the required down payment.

On September 19, 2001—still reeling from the September 11 terrorist attacks on the United States, which had shaken my faith in humankind—I nevertheless attended my university classes. Both attendance and spirits were down, as many students were watching the news or attending discussions on the crisis. After class, I went to Sue Ann's to spend some time with my youngest child, who was not yet in school, before going home to study for a few hours. When I walked in her front door, I immediately sensed that something was different, though everything seemed normal. The familiar noise of children playing echoed through the house. The coffee was on as usual. The scents of Pine Sol and Play-Doh indicated that art time had recently ended. *So, what was different?* I wondered.

Then I looked at Sue Ann's face. In place of her

normally calm demeanor was an intense energy that radiated from where she stood in the kitchen all the way to the foyer. Her eyes danced with an excitement that had nothing to do with the boys having helped clean up the playroom.

She said nothing as she handed me an envelope.

"What is it?" I asked.

"Look inside!"

It was a plain white envelope with Sue Ann's name and address printed neatly on the front. I noticed there was no return address, but thought nothing of it, assuming the sender had simply forgotten to add it. I removed a sheet of paper from the envelope. On it was a child's drawing, in crayon, of a small house, a few stick people, and two trees. *Had my son drawn the picture, or had hers?* I wondered. Either way, I was surprised at her excitement over a picture, even if it was pretty good for a three-year-old.

"There's more!" she said.

I reached inside and pulled out a smaller piece of paper. It was a certified check, drawn on a local bank, with Sue Ann's name typed in as the payee, in the amount of $10,000. Where the sender's name is usually typed, it read, "Anonymous."

I was speechless. Things like that just didn't happen to people like Sue Ann and me. We didn't win the lottery; we never even win the big prizes at bingo.

Finally, I said, "Is this a real check?"

"Yes," she said, beaming. "I called the bank, and they verified that it's for real."

Today, Sue Ann lives in her own house, where she continues to run her child care center. Even with the anonymous gift of $10,000, it was difficult for her to obtain a mortgage, but after months of saving and researching she eventually found a lender and a house. Her new home has two bedrooms on the main floor and a bedroom in the basement. The upper floor is the day care space, with an arts and crafts room, a playroom, and a bedroom for when her charges stay overnight.

Of all the decorative touches that Sue Ann has added to make the house her home, the object that does it best and that draws the most attention is a framed crayon drawing of a house surrounded by trees and a few stick people. Whenever I see that picture on the wall, it reminds me that even in the most tragic and trying of times, there are still people who notice the good and the need in others, and who reach out to make someone else's life a little, or a whole lot, better. And that makes the world a better place for all of us to live in.

—*Danielle R. Gibbings*

To Hold and Behold

My twins were only six weeks old when I found myself in the waiting room of the radiology department at the local hospital. My baby daughter, Abigail, had been born breech, nine minutes after and one and a half pounds lighter than her brother, Daniel. During the delivery, her hip had become dislocated. Now, she needed an X-ray of her hip to make sure that the dislocation had not recurred. The procedure was just a precaution, but I was still nervous.

Abigail's appointment time had come and gone an hour earlier, and I saw no sign that we would be called in for the X-rays soon. The rate of new patients coming in the door far outpaced the rate of people being taken back to the examination rooms.

I made small talk with the other patients, as we all tried to conceal our growing impatience. Many were interested in my babies, and one young woman asked if she could hold Abigail, who was stirring in my arms. I turned her down as politely as I could. Daniel continued to sleep in the double stroller, but I knew it wouldn't be long before he, too, was awake.

A nurse came out and thanked us all for our patience, explaining that they had just finished with the hospital inpatient X-rays for the morning. If we could wait a little longer, they would be with us soon. I hoped she was right, because by then every seat was occupied, except for the one next to me and one across the aisle from me.

Just after the nurse's announcement, the outer door opened and an elderly couple entered the waiting room. They shuffled up to the window and signed in. Together, they turned and glanced about, looking for available seats. I automatically moved the stroller, to allow them room to come sit in the only two remaining vacant seats.

"I'm going to go sit over there by the babies," the man announced loudly.

The lady swatted her husband with her hand and said, "Stop shouting! And don't you bother her; she has her hands full with those babies."

A few people chuckled softly as the elderly couple walked toward me.

The lady took the seat next to me, and her husband took the one across the aisle. He immediately began talking to everyone around him. He was there for a chest X-ray, he said. His doctor wanted him to have it, but he thought it was unnecessary.

"There's nothing wrong with me other than I've been on this earth for eighty-seven years."

His wife clucked at him and scolded him for "bothering everybody," but none of us really minded. We were all restless and bored, and we welcomed his friendly chatter.

He was regaling us with descriptions of his five great-grandchildren when Daniel woke up and began to cry. Tears of my own threatened. Abigail was still kicking and struggling in my arms, and now I had to find a way to pick up Daniel and calm him, too. I felt lost, and then I heard a quiet request.

"Could I hold her for you?"

I hesitated. The elderly lady seated next to me held her arms outstretched. I noticed her hands tremble, and I tried to think of a kind way to refuse her offer without offending her. I couldn't let her hold Abigail, not with her frail and tremulous hands. What if she dropped her?

But instead of politely declining, I found myself handing Abigail to her. I don't recall making the conscious decision to do it, but somehow I was giving my baby daughter to a woman I didn't know.

Abigail kicked and began to wail, and I expected the lady to hand her back to me right away. She didn't. She stroked Abigail's back gently and began to sing to her. I couldn't quite make out the words, but the tune seemed familiar. Abigail quieted almost immediately, and after a few more moments I recognized the song. She was singing "Jesus Loves Me."

I turned my attention to Daniel, cradling him and calming him. Once he'd quieted, I grabbed a cloth from my diaper bag and tried to put it over the lady's shoulder. She shook her head.

"But she'll drool on your blouse," I said.

Her eyes shone brightly and her lip trembled as she spoke, "There's nothing this baby can do to harm my blouse." She turned from me, not wanting me to see her tears, as she rocked my daughter off to sleep.

The woman's husband leaned across the aisle and touched my knee. He was smiling at me, but it was a sad, wistful smile.

"We have five great-grandchildren, you know."

"Yes, you told me," I answered.

He nodded and looked down at his hands in his lap. When he looked back up and met my eyes, I could see that they, too, were brimming with tears.

"Our grandkids won't let us hold any of them, though. I guess they're afraid we'd drop them or something."

I couldn't answer him. I didn't have the words. Moments after he said this, the nurse called for us, and I had to lift Abigail from the lady's arms. After the X-rays had been taken, we left through a different door, so I didn't see the couple again. I'd never even asked their names.

It's been two years since that day in the waiting room. Abigail's X-ray was normal, and she walks now with no ill effects from the hip dislocation she'd suffered at birth. She's still small for her age, still delicate, and still the delight of all that know her.

I pray for that elderly couple nearly every day. Though I don't know where they are or even their names, God knows. And because of them, I now know something, too.

God puts people in our paths for a reason.

Sometimes they are people who need us, so that they may experience the light of God's love shining through another person's soul.

Sometimes they are people whom we need, so as to remind us of God's blessings and abiding love.

And sometimes, like the lady in the waiting room, they are both.

—Adrian R. Ward

The Greatest Man
I Hardly Knew

"What do you remember?" I ask him, truly curious about the past that made this man who he is today: a successful and happily retired business executive, husband, father of six, and grandfather of seventeen.

An easy, lopsided smile dissolves the somberness, and his soft blue eyes glow warm. I wonder why I still feel oddly uncomfortable with him, almost afraid. Is it because he was a symbol of discipline more often than he was a brother, or is the discomfort of my own making, realizing that he surrendered his childhood so I could keep mine?

"I always knew I could outrun you," I tease, plunging in. I remember my tomboyish youth and the belief that my long, lanky legs could outrun anyone.

"I let you think that," he grins, his eyes twinkling as he bites gently on the inside of his lower lip, a trait that has always been a part of him.

We laugh together.

Silence follows, uncomfortable and awkward, until a cloud moves across Louie's face and he begins to speak.

"It was the darkest night I can remember," he says. "Dad came into my room and yanked me out of bed, yelling that I hadn't watered the pigs enough. Then he flung me across the room, swearing that the pigs were out there squealing, keeping him awake."

He told me how scared he was, how he shivered as he stumbled through the pitch-black night in his bedclothes, frightened half to death. Every little sound scared him all the more. It was so dark he couldn't see a thing, but somehow he found the well house and pumped the metal buckets full of water. He tried to feel his way along the path to the pigpens but stumbled over some fallen branches and fell headlong into the empty ditch. Water spilled from the buckets, soaking him. Wet and shivering, he groped his way back to the well house for more water and struggled to do what he had been told. The year was 1942, and Louie had just turned nine years old.

By the age of twelve, he had evolved into being the man of the house. Our abusive father had moved on, taking with him the boy's childhood, leaving behind the overwhelming responsibility of looking out for a mother and three younger siblings. It was a hard life, he admits, getting up before dawn to milk cows, feed the livestock, and cultivate fields, and dashing back to the house for a bite of breakfast and a change of clothes before the school bus came. Sometimes the driver would wait, honking impatiently; other times he would simply drive off, and Louie would walk the mile to school. Then after school there were more chores: machinery to repair, crops to plant or harvest, fields to irrigate—and siblings to discipline.

Alongside our mother, Louie worked our eighty-acre farm. Tractors were a yet-to-be-obtained luxury, so crops were planted and tilled behind horse-drawn machinery. Digging out irrigation ditches was a back-breaking killer of a job, filling and tipping the heavy loads of soil scooped up by a Fresno, a piece of farm equipment used to dig and move earth, pulled by two brawny workhorses, whose reins lay slung across the teenage boy's shoulders. Then there was flood irrigating in the dark of night, when streams were highest and flows the strongest. Always, there lurked the danger of a breakout, which would flood crops nearly ready for harvesting. And harvesting took precedence over everything, even school.

"The winter of forty-eight was a bad one," he says, reminding me that I was only six years old at the time. It was New Year's Eve when the snow began to fall. Winds quickly picked up velocity, forcing people to get home while roads were still passable. By morning, everyone was snowbound.

"We were snowed in nearly four weeks," he explains, pulling up a chair and sitting spraddle-legged across its back. "We made do with what we had. No other choice."

When the skies cleared, people got to town any way they could, whether by horse-drawn sleigh or snowshoes, to load up on supplies. I remember Louie saddling up our roan and strapping burlap bags to the saddle before setting out for town, five miles east. The horse's hooves were wrapped in burlap, too, to help him stay atop the crusted drifts. By late afternoon the winds had returned, but so had Louie, with bags bulging with food. Tucked securely inside his coat was the U.S. mail. He was fifteen years old that year.

"Those were the worst of times," he says thoughtfully, "but some people think they were the best of times." No school, a warm stove to back up against, fresh-baked bread, families bunched around the radio listening to *The Shadow*, while blizzard winds howled outside.

"Do you remember Ferdie?" he asks, changing the subject and laughing at the horrified look flashing across my face.

"How could I forget?" Fragments from old nightmares skittered through my brain, terrifying dreams of a bull from hell storming the house, ready to kill us in our sleep.

Ferdie's Holstein pedigree was magnificent, but to us kids he was Satan himself. Like a creature from a horror novel, the bull was consumed with meanness. We once watched in terror as a workhorse got between him and a heifer he had his sights on. Bellowing with rage, the bull hooked his powerful head under the poor, unsuspecting horse's flanks and flipped him like a feather back over his shoulders. Surprisingly, the horse lived.

An iron nose ring was all that controlled Ferdie—that and the heavy log chain attached to it. But occasionally the chain would slip loose from the ring, and Ferdie would get free. With eyes as blood-red as the Devil's, that terrible behemoth would begin to bawl. With head hung low and swaying, his massive hooves would paw the earth, throwing black dirt up onto his shoulders. His angry bellowing carried for more than a country mile, and the pawing shook the very earth.

"He was pretty scary," Louie laughed. "All I had was a pitchfork and that old leather bullwhip. I expected him to get me every time I stepped into the corral."

With the log chain hanging from his pocket, Louie would enter the corral to face down that hateful animal. By poking with the pitchfork and snapping the fearful whip, Louie would finally get the beast to cower long enough for him to reach in and rehook the chain. It was truly a death-defying act performed more times than I care to remember.

"Tell me about the Civil Air Patrol, how you and Mom helped guard the nation's skies from surprise enemy invasions," I ask.

He sits taller in the chair and tells how a retired Army major introduced him to electronics and taught him Morse code. Together they built a ham radio unit. At fifteen, Louie was a licensed ham operator, talking regularly with operators throughout America and in some foreign countries. Chosen as the youngest ham operator in the state of Idaho, he was awarded a trip to the Civil Air Patrol Convention in Washington, D.C., where he personally met President Harry S. Truman.

"What an honor!" he beams. "That and Boys' State were two of my life's finest achievements."

"Do you remember when I got hurt playing baseball?" he asks, his index finger pressed thoughtfully against his lip.

I remember.

Stretching long and low to snag a hit, he was smashed in the back by a sliding runner. His kidney was badly crushed. The weeks that followed were filled with unbearable pain. He thrashed about in his bed, drenched in perspiration, waging a fierce battle to endure and outlast the intense suffering. My bedroom was adjacent to his, and I can still remember his muffled sobs as he tried to keep us from knowing.

Surgery was scheduled to remove the kidney. As he lay in a Twin Falls hospital the night before, church elders came and gave him a healing blessing. They advised him to rest and not to worry anymore, because the surgery would be unnecessary. Early-morning test results confirmed their prophecy. The kidney had resumed normal functioning during the night, and surgery was no longer needed.

"How come you dropped out of university?" I ask.

"Mom couldn't make it on the farm without me," he replies simply.

When she finally called him for help, he checked out of school and hitchhiked back to Idaho to resume his responsibilities. Years later, after he had married and started a family, he and Mom had to accept the reality that the farm simply could not support two families. Louie left the farm one last time, moving his family to Salt Lake City, where he found work in a gas station and entered trade school. Eventually, he was hired by IBM and moved to California.

"That's where I got really sick," he continues. "My arms started tingling, then my vision blurred and my legs went numb. Doctors diagnosed me with multiple sclerosis. Boy, that pulled the rug out from under me!"

He told of the mental anguish he went through in coming to grips with the devastating possibilities of multiple sclerosis (MS). But only when he had come to terms with it did he tell the rest of us.

"I was stunned when you told us!" I said. "You were supposed to be invincible."

"I was blessed," he laughed. "After aggressive treatment, the MS went into remission and has stayed there since." Once again, his faith carried him through.

My brother and I are older now. It seems easier to talk with him these days than it had been when I was a kid and he was the brother ten years older. I still watch him with a sense of awe, almost a sense of reverence. I wonder if he has any idea how much he impacted my life, especially on one particular day so many years ago?

It was mid-semester of my first year at college. I had caught a ride home for the weekend. No doubt my life was seriously lacking in direction, but I set about blaming everyone else for my misery. I hated school, hated my teachers, hated my classmates. Nothing was worthwhile.

By late afternoon, Louie had had enough. He invited me to ride into town in his cool little hot rod. I was so thrilled I nearly knocked him down in my dash for the car. But as we rode, that old, uncomfortable silence settled between us. To break the silence, I again launched into my "hate life" tirade. With a slight raise of his hand, Louie prompted me to silence. The minutes that followed seemed eternal, and I knew I had crossed the line.

"You know, sis," he said quietly. "If you tell yourself often enough how much you hate something, pretty soon you'll believe it. But it works the other way, too. If you want to like something, tell yourself you'll like it and then you will. What's it going to be?"

Those words seared my brain like a branding iron and later became my life's beacon.

I wonder if he knows he changed my life that day.

—Jean Davidson

Strawberries

As usual, Jean has forgotten our plans and fallen asleep.

"You're such a darling girl; why do you bother with an old lady like me?" Jean mumbles as I nudge her out of bed.

A nurse has dressed her for today's outing in stretch pants, a dotted silk blouse, and a big buttoned sweater that ties at the waist. The salmon-colored lipstick roughly covering her mouth is Jean's own contribution to the outfit.

Luckily, Sequoias' residential coordinator releases Jean without a fuss. I've been treated like a derelict boyfriend ever since I took Jean to a concert and forgot to sign her out. When we returned at 10:00 P.M., giddy as teenagers, the staff had already made out flyers for their escaped inmate.

I'd first met Jean Lado three years earlier, sipping coffee at the intermission of an ethnic dance program. We quickly found our common points: travel, the arts, and a regard for sincerity. Curious about her life, I began visiting Jean. She had a private apartment in the Sequoias then, cluttered with glossy books about the Prado and the pyramids, boxes of hazelnut chocolates she always offered but never ate, reminders to herself that she had begun to forget.

Last year, I returned from a trip abroad to find that Jean had been moved to the facility's health center, after she had been found wandering on the wrong floor. Overnight, Jean's world had shrunk to a starkly furnished room where nurses drifted in and out with pills and meals. Suddenly, I was a "volunteer." I had to give the staff my fingerprints before I could take my friend across the street to St. Mary's Cathedral.

I cringe when people give us a dopey "isn't that sweet, look at the nice young girl and the poor old woman" smile. Especially since I, too, wore that smile at first. I may be a sharp twenty-six-year-old and she a batty ninety-three, but we both need to be needed and loved, a fact I now realize I had denied.

In some ways, I know Jean more intimately than any boyfriend I've had. I've guided her droopy bottom onto the toilet and buttoned up her diapers. One time I came to visit and found Jean in bed naked, her soft, crinkled flesh just oiled by a massage therapist. She looked beautiful—sexy almost—in the openness of her body.

Nobody brings out the good in me like that woman. I'm impatient, an Aries. I run pedestrians off sidewalks with my bicycle. But to touch my heart, all I have to do is try hurrying with Jean.

"You drag me like a sack of potatoes," she'll say, laughing, her dentures slipping as she speaks.

And then I have all the time in the world.

Still, it's hard to stay honest with Jean, knowing lies are lost on her now. I could cancel plans without a call and she'd never know it. To Jean, whether I saw her last month or just yesterday, it's always a lonely eternity.

Jean fantasizes about breaking out of the Sequoias and getting her own San Francisco apartment again.

"I'm useless," she sometimes complains. "I wish I could die, but I am healthy."

In hopes of helping Jean live again, I planned this road trip to Monterey. I take scenic Route 1, where bicyclists roll up green hills and ocean waves smash against rocky cliffs. I stop along the way to collect pinecones, wildflowers, coffee, and strawberries for Jean.

"You treat me like a best boyfriend, like the

Queen of Sheba," she says, gobbling up the whole basket of berries. It's the most I've ever seen Jean eat; she still worries about her weight.

The slow road is a carpet on which Jean's stories unfurl. Like a Zen master, I try to let go of my own tidy version of reality and to follow her drifting mind without judgment.

Sometimes Jean thinks we are on a Sunday drive through Westchester, New York, where she lived when she joined her brother in America. There, she met and married a Hungarian businessman. By then, Jean was too old to bear children, her lifelong regret. Ten years later, a heart attack suddenly killed Michael as he lay on their couch. That day is an island in Jean's memory, a story she repeats with exactitude.

Today, I draw some childhood stories out of Jean. She grew up in Minsk, Russia, surrounded by orchards and forests that supplied the family lumber business. Jean cried when her father cut down trees. She cried so much that her mother used to say she was "born on a wet spot."

It took months before Jean took down the fence around this part of her past. Around gentiles like me, she pretends to be French Catholic—the identity she took on when her family fled to Paris during World War II—rather than a Russian Jew. She says her real name is Henriette, but that Americans have trouble dropping the silent *H*. It's all a piece of the mystery that draws me to Jean. *Who was this lady? Who is she now? Who am I, when I am beside her?*

I got to explore Jean's past when her lawyer, Bob Bockleman, drove me in his army-green Cadillac to her storage space way out in Hunter's Point. I had wanted to pull out some things to make Jean's room at the Sequoias look more like a home than a hospital. Like reading a lover's diary, it was a sick thrill exploring those artifacts, clues to Jean's former life. Yellowed hand-embroidered handkerchiefs, letters from France and the Philippines, spiral notebooks scribbled with to-do lists and vocabulary words, a black velvet coat Jean surely wore to the symphony. I took home a stash of photos—Jean cuddling a puppy in the Russian countryside, skiing in the Swiss Alps, walking Central Park in a smart suit. They were dots I could pretend to connect to a whole.

Jean is telling her stories with closed eyes.

"Look at the ocean," I command.

She opens her eyes, startled. "Oh, being with you is like a dream. I cannot open my eyes."

She's a walking book of such one-liners, from "A friend in need is a friend, indeed" to "You are like a candy—so sweet I want to eat you up." "Cold hands, warm heart" is her trademark phrase, though I'm not sure she knows it. Since we have dug Russia from the bottom of her mind, today she pulls out one of her mother's favorite sayings: "Live a hundred years, study a hundred years, and die like a stupid."

Jolted from her memories, now she's glancing nervously at her watch, every few minutes asking how much farther. Perhaps we've gone too far. Jean has talked to me about traveling for so long that I have come to trust her schemes.

"I will follow you to Paris like a *somnambule*, a sleepwalker!" she likes to say, eyes twinkling. But though she resents her cage, when someone opens its door, she's scared to death to step outside it. "It is windy today," she'll say, if I suggest a walk outdoors.

When we finally reach the Monterey Bay Aquarium, we end up skimming the displays. It's hard squeezing past the crowds to get near the tanks, and Jean has trouble deciphering their contents. To her eyes, barnacles are eggs, sea anemones are rocks, and a tank of sponges and corals is one strange creature.

"There is so much to study here, it would take too much time," Jean says.

I take Highway 101, the quick route, back, as it is dark and Jean is tired.

She gives me a goodnight kiss back at the Sequoias. "I had a lovely time, my sweetie," she says, "But there's no place like home."

This will be Jean's last trip, as her death wish

begins to unfurl four months later. Cancer spreads from her fallopian tubes, poisoning her entire body. Jean alternates between mean and sweet, like a switch. She drinks only coffee and eats only strawberries. She yells in French when she speaks at all.

If I hadn't glimpsed an earlier version of Jean, I doubt I could appreciate anything about her present state, blurred by confusion, pain, and drugs. But there are moments of grace, when Jean breaks the silence with a boisterous howl, when her lips accept a strawberry from my fingers. And at those moments, a spark of love transcends us both.

—*April Thompson*

Sisters in Time

I wondered whether I was a failure as a Big Sisters volunteer. Over forty, full of adult responsibilities, and with children of my own, what was I giving Amber that was of any value? I couldn't understand her life.

Amber was quiet with me. When she did speak, she kept her head down.

At seven years old, she often had her fingers, fist, or shirt in her mouth. Her skin was mahogany dark, her features perfect. When she did lift her chin, her bright eyes gave away nothing. Her skin had a smooth matte finish that seemed not to reflect your gaze, but to pull you in. If you saw a picture of just her face, you might think her to be twenty-seven.

I liked Amber, but I didn't like to pick her up at her home. No matter how many times I called to remind her I was coming, she was never ready. Her small house was full of aunts, uncles, cousins, and chaos. Amber was always looking for a shoe, a coat, a swimsuit, or something needed for our outing. Her grandmother was kind to me; the scads of children talked to me cautiously and then returned to their rambunctious play.

Amber did not run to me and hug me when I came to pick her up; she didn't thank me when I dropped her off. At the end of each visit, I'd ask her, "What was your favorite part of our time together?" She always mumbled back, "Everything." Sometimes that one word was her only word on our ride back to her house. That one word kept me coming back.

When she did talk, she often told me things I didn't believe.

"I got suspended for fighting, but the teacher told me to hit the other kid."

"My grandma said to meet her at the ice-cream store, so you have to take me there."

"I don't have to do homework."

She also told me things I believed.

"No, I don't have any gloves. I had some, but I can't keep anything in my house. My house is crazy with too many people."

"Yes, I liked the shirts you got me for Christmas. They were the only long-sleeved shirts I had all winter, but they're getting small for me."

I was careful not to buy her too much; I'd been

cautioned against this by the Big Sisters social worker. I did buy ten pairs of gloves at the dollar store, and I gave her a new pair every time I saw her that winter. I found clothes from my now-grown daughter in the attic and gave Amber a few things each time I saw her. I couldn't bring peaceful order to her life, but I could try to meet some simple needs.

Her family kept her hair beautifully braided. "My auntie comes over Thursdays and braids all our hair." Her clothes were clean and well matched. They had a tree at Christmas and a pot of petunias on the front porch in the summer. Between them, the extended family tried to give these children a good life.

I never understood the identity of all the relatives that came and went, and after a while I gave up trying. I just knew that some stayed a while, and some dropped off their kids and left. Some came by to cook dinner, to cut the grass, or to shoo all the kids out and scrub the floors.

After a year of planned outings—bowling, miniature golf, movies, dinners—and games, I wondered if I'd done anything for Amber that really made a difference in her life. On my way to pick her up one crisp November afternoon, I was feeling guilty that my life was so busy that I had to take her with me to get my oil changed and then to the grocery store before we could go to my house to make homemade pizza together.

The same scene greeted me when I arrived to pick her up. Her small kitchen was full of people, yelling to the hallway, "Amber, get your coat. Find your other shoe. Your Big Sister is here." The house felt crowded and hot, so I said I'd wait outside, after reminding one of the aunts that Amber should bring along her homework.

Amber didn't appear for ten minutes, enough time for me to think about our year of outings. Some months earlier, I had decided not to constantly correct Amber and, instead, on each visit I'd try to teach Amber one thing using a more positive approach. I remembered how once I'd told her, "You have such a beautiful face, but I can't see it when you put your hands in your mouth." I realized that she didn't put her hands in her mouth anymore. Then I remembered that the lies had stopped after I'd said, "The folks at Big Brothers/Big Sisters matched us because we're both smart. You can't fool me." And she was holding her head up now.

She didn't hug me when she came out the door, but I did get a "hello" and a faint smile.

The oil change took more than an hour. As we waited, I helped her with her homework and we went through the papers in her backpack. We talked about the colors she'd used in a painting and how confusing subtraction is when you have to do a lot of borrowing. I checked my watch several times. The oily smell seemed to remind me that this was no place for a special outing.

I didn't feel much better about our activity at the grocery store, until some unusual things happened—unusual for Amber, that is. She seemed carefree, almost excited. I had to remind her not to run in the store. Then she skipped. Once, while we were talking about what kind of cheese to buy, she gently squeezed my hand. She must be excited about making pizza, I thought. Perhaps cooking together will be a breakthrough.

When we got to my home, she worked with me to roll out the dough. The rest of my family joined us. We all made our own little individual pizzas and played a game of Uno together before I took Amber home.

Amber was, as usual, quiet on the drive back. I asked, "What was your favorite part of our time together?"

She answered in a split second, "The car place." She took a gulp of air. "I liked the time with just you and me."

I glanced in the rearview mirror, and her eyes were already there, ready to meet mine. "I liked that, too," I answered.

During the rest of the ride home, we were silent and happy in each other's presence. As we walked to her house, I asked if I could give her a hug. She turned and wrapped her arms around me, then quickly bolted to the door. As she grabbed the knob, she turned her head toward me. Her eyes met mine again. We both saw each other's tears. She ran back and gave me one more hug. Fast as a lightning strike, she was gone. She disappeared into her busy home full of people who loved her.

We were of different races and separated by almost four decades. We lived in different parts of the city and lived different lives. But our time together had brought us to a new understanding. We knew then that we were sisters. We still are.

—*Amy Jenkins*

Close Encounters of
the Best Kind

Five years ago, when I had a nine-to-five job, I commuted to work—two to three hours to the office, four to five hours home. I did that every day for three full years. I've got the stubs from the bus companies to prove it.

I no longer schlep to an office like a regular working Jane, and these days I rarely take the bus anywhere. Although those long, grueling hours of traveling are far behind me, I still carry with me the priceless gifts of three complete strangers.

And I met them all while riding a bus.

It was my first day back to work after a month-long illness, and my first time to ride a bus in as long. As I waited at the bus stop, I wondered whether I'd luck out and get a seat. I wasn't a woman who expected a man to offer his seat to me; after all, we all paid the same fare. But I didn't relish the thought of having to stand the entire trip dressed in office clothes and high heels, especially since I still felt weak from the illness.

That morning, I stepped inside the crowded bus and wanted to just turn around, get off, go home, and call in sick. Maybe it was the panic on my face, or maybe I turned a pale shade of green, but before I could bolt, a man stood up and offered me his seat. I thanked him and gratefully sat down. As the bus rumbled through the city streets, jolting its passengers with each stop and start and every corner, we talked and discovered that we both worked in the same area, our office buildings only two blocks away from each other. He stood the whole way . . . for two hours.

Until then, I'd rarely seen, much less experienced, such chivalry. There are those who would have us believe that chivalry has gone out of fashion, but my experience on the bus that day convinced me otherwise. I was, and still am, grateful to have been on the receiving end of it. And I've made a point of practicing the ageless custom of chivalry, in my own way, with simple acts of kindness to others, whenever and wherever I can.

Most of the time during my commuting days, I smiled a lot. I smiled at the person next to me on the bus and across from me. I smiled at the security guard at the office building where I worked. I smiled at the janitor as he mopped the hallway floor. I smiled at the cashier in the mall.

Smiling at people became second nature for me, a genuine expression that came spontaneously from my heart. But at first, I did it because I had learned that if I smiled at someone, I'd get a smile in return. An old woman taught me that lesson, and I didn't even know her.

I was seated beside her on the bus on my way to work one morning. She had kind eyes and kept looking out the window, *ooohing* and *aaahing* at the tall buildings and sights.

I was trying to read a book, and she kept leaning over my seat, causing me to lose my concentration. I was about to ask her if she wanted to trade seats, but the look of wonder on her face stopped me. Her eyes were wide and shining, and her mouth was stretched in a wide smile.

She was oblivious to my stare, because her eyes were fixed on something outside: a section of skyway still under construction. She seemed delighted at the sight of cars and buses going up the ramp and onto the skyway.

I couldn't help but feel somewhat envious of her joy. I'd seen those same buildings, same skyways, same scenes countless times before, but never in the way and with the delight she did. I was humbled that she found something so simple, which I had considered to be mundane, to smile about.

I turned to her and saw that she was looking at me, the smile gone from her lips. I wanted to see her smile again, yet I was unsure of what to do. Finally, in the passing of a split second, I decided to take the risk: I smiled.

She smiled back. And I saw that the glow had returned to her wrinkled face.

I've been smiling at people ever since . . . on the bus, in the market, on the street, and everywhere in my life. Most of the time, they smile back.

It was a warm March evening, and I'd just taken a seat on the bus that would take me home. I sat in the third row, by the window, on the driver's side. It was nearly 6:00 P.M., but the bus was not yet full and the driver gave no indication that he intended to get the bus on the road anytime soon.

A middle-aged woman took a seat opposite me. She was crying. Not speaking to anyone in particular, she tearfully narrated her story.

She had come to the city to visit her daughter. On the way to the terminal, a thief had snatched one of her bags. It had contained half of the money she'd brought with her. The other half was rolled in a hankie and hidden under her blouse, so she fortunately still had some money left.

The bus conductor, driver, and other passengers listened to her tale. After a few minutes, she stopped crying, removed some cheese bread from her bag, and began to eat, worry still knitting her brow.

An old man in tattered clothes got on the bus. He sat in the seat directly in front of the woman.

After a few minutes, all seats were taken. The driver got behind the wheel and started the engine. The bus conductor collected tickets and began asking us where we were getting off. When he came to the old man's seat, he became suspicious and asked the old man whether he had any money. The old man admitted that he did not. He explained that he had spent all his money that morning when he'd accidentally got on the wrong bus and now he was trying to go home.

Upon hearing this, the bus conductor ordered the old man to get off the bus. The old man didn't budge. He was almost in tears as he begged the bus conductor to let him take that bus so he could get home before dark. The bus driver, who had been listening to the exchange, stood up, approached the old man, and repeated the conductor's command to get off the bus.

The woman seated behind the old man was also listening and observing the incident. When the bus driver and conductor raised their voices at the old man, she interfered.

"Stop harassing him! Can't you see he's only trying to get home?"

"He doesn't have any money!" the driver shouted.

"Well, that's no reason to throw him off the bus," she insisted.

Then she said, "How much is his fare?"

The bus conductor mumbled the amount.

"Fine," said the woman. She reached inside her blouse, took out her remaining money, and handed the fares to the bus conductor. "Here's his fare and mine. Just stop giving him a hard time."

All heads turned to the woman, who, just minutes before, had been crying over the money she'd lost.

"It's only money," she shrugged.

By the time the bus rolled out of the terminal, she had given the old man some of her bread and a dollar. She rode the rest of the way home wearing a Mona Lisa smile of peace and grace, the money she'd lost earlier forgotten.

On the road of life, the chivalry and smiles of strangers can lighten our loads and lift our spirits. How much sweeter the journey when we make it a little smoother and richer for others.

—*Shery Ma Belle Arrieta*

Roots for Sofia

Ten-year-old, going on thirty, Sofia de la Paz Flores carefully weighed her words before pitching her plan for an orchard behind her home.

The thin slice of backyard, perhaps five feet square, in the community of La Panamá clings to the edge of a precipice. The rocky ravine far below is littered with garbage and crosscut by a polluted stream. Julie Dunsmore, the Presbyterian Disaster Assistance (PDA) mission coworker accompanying me, reminded Sofia that a fence was planned to protect small children from the danger.

Sofia was quick to suggest a gate.

Julie laughed, complimenting the girl on her persistence. Julie and her husband work as liaisons between PDA and A-Brazo (a play on the Spanish words for arm and hug), an ecumenical Christian organization promoting self-development by providing safe, affordable housing for El Salvador's most vulnerable—the poor, particularly earthquake refugees like Sofia and her mother.

"It's only a few trees," Sofia pleaded, with her doe-eyed attempt at coercion.

Sofia's mother, Maria, remained silent. As Julie and I surveyed the area, she continued to wield a shovel like a prod, demanding the earth to cooperate with her aspirations.

Clearly there was no place to plant trees. It was a less-than-ideal building site to begin with. But these dusty eight and a half acres were obviously paradise to the 210 families who had chosen to build there.

Thousands of others still remained in temporary housing almost two years after the 7.8 tremor that had left them homeless. More than 200 additional families (many of them friends and relatives of the new residents of La Panamá) were still stranded on a nearby soccer field, desperately hoping for another piece of land, like the one in La Panamá, to become available.

Land is at a premium in this mountainous country not much bigger than Massachusetts, and homeownership is beyond the imagination of most of El Salvador's poor. Sofia and her mother were among the fortunate few to be chosen to participate in this Presbyterian Disaster Assistance project. La Panamá is a prototype community, a project desperately needed in a city plagued by poverty and crime.

Maria Flores understood that reality. Cinderblock by cinderblock and with each shovelful of cement, she was gratefully paying off her mortgage in sweat equity. She was the one I had come to interview.

Maria and her only child, Sofia, had survived a landslide that had taken most of their neighborhood, as well as the lives of friends and family. She echoed the story I'd heard a hundred times before from other survivors of Central America's cyclical natural disasters. El Salvador barely survived a civil war, only to be lashed by the category five Hurricane Mitch, which devastated most of Central America in 1998. On the heels of that disaster, came the earthquake that had left the Flores family homeless.

I'd heard many similar stories of loss, harrowing bravery, and shattered hope bolstered by unswerving resilience. I admired the *damnificados* (damaged ones), as they called themselves, but I had become almost calloused to their tales of woe.

"How did you go on?" I asked. "You lost your home, your job—everything."

How did any of them get up morning after morning, to face another day of destitution on an overcrowded soccer field in the tarp-and-tin ghetto they'd called home for almost two years? The government had made promises, but the government was always making promises it couldn't keep.

"From where did your strength come?" I persisted.

But Maria just crossed her arms and stared past me.

"Tell me about the trees," I braved, recalling the urgency in Sofia's request.

The beginning of a wry smile deepened the lines around Maria's mouth and the fine wrinkles at the outer corners of her eyes.

I complimented her daughter, impressed by Sofia's intelligence, quick wit, and dogged persistence in pursuit of the desires of her heart. "She will go far," Julie and I agreed.

Maria nodded, the glimmer of motherly pride just below the surface of weary black eyes.

"The trees gave us hope," she said, meeting my gaze.

Over the course of a few years, Maria had purchased twenty-five seedlings from her barely subsistent wages as a laborer on a governmental project in mosquito control. One at a time, she'd purchased mango, cashew, avocado, mamey, lime, orange, and paterna seedlings. Mother and daughter planted hope in plastic containers that graced their rented *champa*, a wood-and-tin shack in a poor neighborhood less than two miles from La Panamá.

"*Mi jardin.*" My garden. A broad grin lit her eyes.

"But why not a flower garden?"

"Sofia needed strong roots."

Marie's seedlings became, along with pineapple

hedges and banana trees, the down payments on a dream: a house with a garden and an orchard.

"I watered them every morning," she said. "And they watered my soul."

This morning ritual had inspired Maria before the earthquake, for she had long dreamed of the house she would one day own. After the earthquake, the ritual became her lifeline.

"They were my prayer," Maria said softly.

Mother and daughter had carried each tree one by one from the wreckage of the landslide to the soccer field more than a mile away. The seedlings flourished and bloomed during the long, agonizing months in the temporary shelter. When Maria and Sofia rode in the truck to their new home in La Panamá, they held the precious seedlings in their laps. Now, the tiny trees were ready to put down roots.

Aching for their dream of an orchard to be fulfilled, I implored, "Is there no place to plant the trees?"

Maria smiled. "We will plant them along the streets of La Panamá. They will provide shade for everyone."

Then she added, "We are home now."

—*Roberta B. Updegraff*

I Won't Forget

When I see a stranger staring at me through my window, I just naturally get nervous.

It was past closing time on a cold, windy January night, but the little gas stove in the corner kept the place warm. Having cleaned the griddle, washed the dishes, and swept the floor, I hesitated before throwing out the half-pot of coffee. At a nickel a cup, I'd be wasting at least two bits' worth. So, I locked the door, poured a cup, and sat down to keep an eye on the stranger. He didn't move. I thought about calling someone but remembered the unpaid phone bill.

Located on a dead-end street next to the tracks, my little hamburger joint sat apart from other buildings. The nearest streetlight was a block away. I didn't usually feel this isolated, but that night I had a bad case of the heebie-jeebies. An eastbound freight had just come through town, and I had seen enough hoboes hanging around to make me leery.

I wondered whether any of the previous owners of this little one-man business had felt this way when they closed up late. By my count, five students before me had worked their way through school by owning and operating the infamous College Inn.

I was about to empty the pot and wash it when Blocker pulled up to the door in his new Ford and honked. Good old Blocker! He stood six-foot-three and weighed in at 290 pounds. I couldn't have asked for a more welcome customer.

Relieved, I stuck my head out the door. "Come on in, Hoss. No curb service tonight. It's too cold."

The car's springs squeaked gratefully as he stepped out. "Hey, Willy," he said. "Do you have a copy of your notes for the geology test tomorrow? I just dropped Dolphia off at the dorm and I need to study."

"Yeah, here they are." I pulled a folder from my backpack and handed it to him.

He said, "Why are you open so late, anyway?"

"A lot of guys at the dorm are up studying for finals. They're always hungry, and I cooked up a couple of dozen burgers to sell. I'm about ready to close."

Blocker looked out the window. "Who's that skinny little guy standing out there in the dark?"

I looked out at the man. He didn't seem nearly as menacing as before. Hatless, he clutched a thin, worn jacket to his bony chest. A cardboard suitcase with a piece of rope tied around it rested at his feet. The wind whipped his pant legs and ruffled his hair. He looked miserable.

I tried to appear unconcerned. "I was just about to invite him in for a cup of coffee when you drove up," I lied.

Blocker looked out at the lonely figure and shouted, "Hey, mister! Come on in and get warm."

The man picked up his bag and quickly entered the little one-room café. "Thanks," he said, warming his hands at the stove. "I hadn't planned on stopping here, but a railroad cop threw me off the train." He accepted a cup of coffee and sipped noisily. "Where am I, anyway?"

"You're in Alpine, Texas, man." Blocker spread his arms. "A hundred miles from nowhere and home of Sul Ross State Teachers College. Where you headed?"

"South Texas. I had a streak of hard luck out in Arizona. I've got kinfolks down in the valley, and they've promised me a job."

"What kind of work do you do?"

"Mechanic."

I noticed him eyeing the sack of food. "Are you hungry? I've got some burgers here."

He licked his lips. "I haven't eaten all day."

"Gotta go, Willy." Blocker walked to the door. "Thanks for the notes."

"Bring them by my room when you're finished. I'll be up late."

After Blocker left I watched the stranger devour the burger. "I don't suppose you have a place to sleep tonight," I said.

"No, I don't."

I walked to a closet and retrieved a bedroll. "I can't put you out on a night like this. You can sleep here if you'd like."

"Oh, my God. I can't begin to . . ." Emotion filled his voice. "Thank you, sir." He stared at the floor. "Maybe I could sweep . . ."

"It's okay, I already did that," I said. "You just get some sleep. There'll be another freight stopping here around daylight. Maybe you can catch it."

Watching the stranger cautiously, I emptied the cash register, the jukebox, and the pinball machine. I said goodnight and locked the door. Then I proceeded to the dorm to sell my burgers and get in some studying.

I told Reed, my roommate, about my experience.

"Are you crazy?" he said. "That guy will rob you blind!"

"I worried about that," I said. "But there's not much in there he can steal, and he seemed so . . ."

"You're an idiot." He crawled into bed. "And turn down that radio."

"Okay, okay." I sat at my desk and hit the books.

It was barely daylight when a train whistle woke me. Reed was still asleep. I thought about what he had said and hurried down to the café.

The man was gone. The coffeepot had been washed and turned upside-down on the rack. A clean cup sat beside it. The bedroll was tied and put away neatly in the closet. Then I found the note.

On a napkin in scrawling, childish handwriting were the words, "You are a good man. I won't forget."

Corpus Christi, Texas—Eleven Years Later

"Bye, honey. I'll call you as soon as my meeting is over." I kissed Margaret and gave her a hug. "Kiss Libbie for me when she wakes up. Tell her Daddy will bring her something from San Antonio."

It was early morning, still dark. A rare cold front had passed through during the night and a strong, dry wind rustled the oleanders by the carport. As I guided the Dodge down Lexington Avenue and along the highway, I sipped hot coffee from a Styrofoam cup. My appointment with the oil company was for nine o'clock, and I knew I'd be cutting it close.

When the sun peeked over the horizon, I was rehearsing my pitch to the oil company people when a loud thump sounded under the hood, accompanied by a lot of rattles and eerie squeals. I pulled over and raised the hood. A busted fan belt! I looked around, wondering what to do. A sign pointing down a side road announced, "George West, Texas." I decided to risk it and cautiously drove in that direction, hoping I could get to a garage before I blew a head gasket.

The radiator was boiling and weird sounds were coming from under the hood, but to my relief, I soon saw a sign that read "AUTO REPAIR," and pulled in.

The place was closed, but there was an emergency number. So, I turned off the hissing motor, walked across the highway to a diner, and made the call.

A woman's sleepy voice answered the phone. She said she'd wake her husband.

Soon, a pickup arrived. A heavyset man emerged, and I told him my problem.

"Go back over to the café and have a cup of coffee," he said. "I shouldn't be long."

I was just finishing up a plate of bacon and eggs when the mechanic came in and sat down at the counter beside me. He ordered coffee.

"How much do I owe you?" I said.

"You ever run a café in Alpine?"

Surprised, I said, "Yes."

"Then you don't owe me anything. And your breakfast is on me."

I looked at his face for a moment and then smiled.

"I didn't recognize you. You must have caught that train."

"Yeah, I caught it, and I've put on a few pounds since that night. Eating regularly will do that."

"How long has it been? Ten years?"

"Eleven. I don't forget things like that."

—*William M. Barnes*

Ruthie's Run

The morning sun sat low on the horizon, reflecting from the windows of our big yellow school bus as it bounced along the blacktop of the two-lane prairie highway. My eight-year-old sister, Ruthie, and I were on board, traveling with the rest of Ruthie's public school track team, bound for the county meet fifty miles away. It was not my idea of fun, but a previous commitment had prevented Mom and Dad from chaperoning Ruthie, and I had been drafted as her escort.

Don't get me wrong. I enjoy track. I run the anchor on my school's junior 400-meter relay team. Besides, it's a great way to meet guys. I even like Ruthie. When you're fifteen and it's June, though, every Saturday is a must day for hanging out with your friends—not with your little sister. So, of course, I tried to beg off.

But, as Mom reminded me when she dragged me out of bed at the crack of dawn, being a big sister has its responsibilities as well as its privileges. So there I was, stuck on a bus with a bunch of grade schoolers, heading for a lost Saturday. Ruthie, at least, was excited.

The meet was a first for her. She craned her neck at every passing landmark, chattered like a chipmunk, and wriggled in her seat in anticipation of the day's events. She was thrilled not only because she had qualified for her first big track meet, but also because she expected to see some of the out-of-town friends she had made at Brownie camp the summer before. By the time we arrived at the athletic field, the sun had risen higher in the clear Alberta sky and the early summer heat was beginning to build over the track. I set up a private cheering section in the shade of the bleachers, and Ruthie went off exploring. Sure enough, she met some of her Brownie buddies, including her special friend, Susan. Their friendship was special, because Susan had helped Ruthie to conquer her fear of water and learn to swim the previous summer, while others had taunted and teased. Ruthie had never forgotten Susan's kindness.

The girls spent time catching up on the year's news, and when the talk turned to the present, Ruthie discovered that she and Susan would be participating in the same event: the 400-meter run, once around the big high school track. It was a tough test for novice runners, but Ruthie knew she could do it, and knowing her friend would be running with her made her feel even better.

The meet began, and Ruthie spent most of the morning following her friends and cheering them on. When the officials broke for lunch, she rejoined me to share the picnic basket our mom had packed. As we munched our sandwiches and washed them down with jars of Ruthie's secret fuel, water from our well, we talked about her strategy for the race.

Ruthie had trained hard, running for miles around the wheat fields on our farm, and her qualifying times were very good. This was a step up, though, and the competition would be stiff. She promised me she would do her very best and reminded me that the race would be even more fun because Susan was running, too! The events got under way again, and Ruthie ran off to rejoin her friends. Finally, late in the afternoon, they called the tyke girls' 400-meter runners to the line. Ruthie reappeared beside me. I tightened the laces on her running shoes and hugged her for luck, and she hurried over to the start to join the other runners, including Susan.

At the starting line, she and Susan stood side by side, one in red shorts, the other in blue, their legs flexing nervously as they listened carefully to the instructions. Taking their marks, the two friends rose in tandem to the set position and froze like statues until the sharp crack of the starter's gun set them free. The pack broke together, cinders flying, as the inexperienced runners sprinted toward the first turn, jockeying for position, each fighting for the lead. I knew they couldn't maintain that furious pace for long, and sure enough, as they came out of the turn, the group slowed and two figures, one in red shorts, the other in blue, began to pull away. Running stride for stride, they pushed each other down the backstretch and left the others well behind.

Locked in their own private battle, with arms and legs driving like pistons, Ruthie and Susan powered into the far turn, still neck and neck. Blue shorts on the inside, red on the outside, the duel continued at a cruel pace. Something had to give. And it did.

Susan reached the limit of her endurance. Her stride grew choppy, she began to falter, and Ruthie started to move ahead. My heart leaped with hope as Ruthie swept out of the final corner, five meters in front, running free and easy. Susan trailed, running doggedly now, fighting exhaustion, trying to stay in the race.

The cheering crowd came to its feet, yelling encouragement, and Ruthie's lead widened to ten and then to twenty meters. As she neared the finish, the hint of a smile appeared on Ruthie's determined face, and she glanced over her shoulder to place her opponents. Suddenly, she broke stride. Her pace slowed and then, unbelievably, she stopped, just short of the beckoning chalk line.

Ruthie stood there, looking back up the track, bent slightly at the waist, panting with exertion. The triumphant look on her face had faded, replaced with one of concern. Susan was crying. Still running, now with her right hand clutching a stitch in her side and tears of pain streaking her face, she struggled to finish.

The crowd of onlookers began to call to Ruthie, urging her to run, and her coach started yelling at her, demanding she cross the line. But Ruthie stood fast. She waited for her friend, and then, with hips touching and arms around each other's shoulders, they jogged the last few strides and broke the tape together.

The officials were in a dither. Protests were lodged, and meetings were held. Ultimately, both girls were disqualified for interference, and the ribbons went to others. Ruthie's coach chided her, and her simple act of kindness and friendship was held up to ridicule. I hugged Ruthie my hardest ever that day, and warned away the others with the anger in my eyes. You see, the adults just didn't understand. But Susan did, and I did. And when I told my parents, they did, too. Because we knew Ruthie, and we knew that in life's long run, Ruthie was and would always be a winner!

I will always remember that day, when an unwelcome assignment became a lesson in life and later a cherished memory. You see, Ruthie went on to achieve athletic success and to experience the thrill of victory many times and in many sports before, at the age of seventeen, she was killed by a drunk driver. Her high school retired her sweater number, and I was given custody of her ribbons and trophies. I treasure them.

But to this day, I'm still proudest of the ribbon my little sister didn't win on that prairie track many Saturdays ago.

—John Forrest, as told by Ruthie's sister,
who wishes to remain anonymous.

Here and Now,
If Not Always

As we approach the elementary school, Juanito's* little hand grasps my larger one. His fingers tighten until the fingernails dig small moons into my hand.

I am the eighth mother for my six-year-old foster son. When he arrived at my house, a lone plastic grocery bag held his only links to the past: three pairs of blue jeans, three T-shirts, three pairs of socks, four pairs of underpants, a pair of pajamas, and a handful of small plastic army men.

In his time with me, Juanito has confronted a new town, a new house, and a new foster parent. And new water. ("It doesn't taste like water in that other city—whatchacallit.") New food. ("But I don't like your salad. This lettuce tastes icky.") New rules. ("But that other foster mom—what was her name? She let me stay up all night.") He's having to cope with two new dogs. A new brand of toothpaste. ("Pretty good, actually.") And a bedroom filled with unfamiliar shadows.

He gropes for light switches in the kitchen, rummages through four dresser drawers to find the one that holds his socks, struggles to extricate himself from the seat belt in this confusing new world.

Yet, he's settling in. An ice cream cone brings a wan smile to his lips. An occasional giggle ripples from his throat when I flutter a butterfly kiss onto his cheek at bedtime. In rare moments between the storms that accompany bathing and getting ready for bed, his brown eyes sparkle and the dark circles underneath fade. Hugs, toys, and treats from a virtual stranger eager to love him are not enough to erase the trauma of this move or to stanch the wounds from so much loss, but they provide momentary respite from the pain.

As we step into the bustling school where hundreds of tiny people mill about my knees, I realize that my leap from an unattached single woman to a foster mother has dramatically altered my life, too.

I no longer sip cappuccino while debating the meaning of life with philosopher friends, attend happy-hour gatherings to discuss the state of the planet with colleagues, or participate in local political events. I am too immersed in cooking grilled cheese sandwiches, singing nursery rhymes, bandaging skinned knees, and finding lost shoes to indulge in the frivolous pursuits that used to captivate me.

Instead of slipping out to a movie with a friend, I spend my time with Juanito. Together we try to unravel the deeper mysteries of the world. As Juanito marvels at the clouds sweeping past the moon on a star-filled night, I join him in wondering why. When we chance upon a fuzzy worm during an outing to the zoo, we wonder what. As we study the makeup on a clown at the circus, we wonder who. And as we watch mothers shepherd their children through the grocery store, push swings at the city park, and distribute hamburgers to smiling broods at McDonalds, we retreat into ourselves to ponder the most important questions of all: where, when, and for how long. . . .

Where will the bureaucratic wheel that has caught half a million children in its spokes send him the next time it turns? When will Juanito's mother choose him over drugs and build the kind of life that has room for a small boy? If her parental rights are terminated, as the social workers hope, and he joins the tens of thousands of children in the United States awaiting adoption, will a family come forward to choose him? How long will he be mine to love?

Today, as I walk Juanito to his new classroom, the small hand clutching mine whispers the answers: here and now, if not always. The security of tomorrow is what he truly needs, but any mom can chase the shadows from a youngster's day. As I give his hand a reassuring squeeze, I feel honored that, for the time being, it is me.

—Linda Sonna

*The child's name and identifying information have been changed.

Reglar Feller

immie Joe Thomas was a reglar feller, he used to assure me, just like you and me. But I could see differences. For one, I dressed better than he did. For another, he had more money than I could ever hope to have. But he never patronized me. When we went out drinking, we took turns paying for drinks. He gave my opinions, when I offered them, the same weight as those from his lawyer or his banker—probably more weight than those of his lawyer, because he had no abiding love for those "bottom fishers," as he called them.

Out-of-towners who saw him in his bib overalls and denim shirt as he walked the railroad right-of-way usually mistook him for a gandy dancer checking the tracks. Locals all knew he owned the railroad. A time had come a while back when shipping rates threatened to destroy Jimmie Joe's ability to meet competitors' prices on the furniture produced at his factory. Not one for long hassles and prolonged haggling, he up and bought the railroad. After that, he used the railway to bring in raw materials as well as to carry out finished furniture. The increase in business brought down the costs at his furniture plant enough to where he added more workers and also brought down his shipping rates to where rival furniture makers starting shipping on his train line.

Jimmie Joe soon discovered that a railroad consumes large quantities of coal, which costs large amounts of money to buy. So when the local coal yard was on its last legs and ready to lay off workers, he stepped in and bought it, too. Of course, his trains not only hauled in coal for both his railroad and his furniture factory, but also for other businesses and homes in the area.

"I ain't got nothin agin book larning," Jimmie Joe once told me. "There just warn't enough money coming in to keep us, so I quit school and got a job. I kin hire college boys now, so I just cain't see the need to go back fur any edjication."

He started in the furniture factory as a floor sweeper and moved up the ladder quickly. With his fast mind and analytic ability, he worked out better ways to do things—things that had been done the same way for years. When he started to earn a more comfortable wage, he married the factory owner's daughter.

Sara Jane, his love light, fitted well into his life. She gave him three home-cooked meals a day as well as the love and encouragement that make the difference between a successful man and a happy-as-a-king successful man. Better educated than her husband, Sara Jane could talk intelligently about books, music, and philosophy—but never in front of Jimmie Joe. People around them always saw her in a stiffly starched house dress, scented slightly with bath soap and wisteria, taking freshly baked cookies to a schoolroom or home-cooked meals to shut-ins. Not once did anyone ever hear her advise her husband on any subject; still, her presence could be seen in all his enterprises.

Jimmie Joe frequently contributed articles to *Furniture South,* the regional magazine of the industry. It was my job to clean up his writing and correct his grammar. Some other "self-made" men in his position resented a single change to their work. "Do whatever it needs to make it fitten to print," Jimmie would say.

When the union sent in organizers to organize the plant, they found little support from the workers. A few, those who had been let go after many unsuccessful tries to help them fit in, did join the cause. When Jimmie Joe looked out his office window and saw the picketers in front of the plant, he exploded, "That's a damn shame!"—whereupon, he had a trailer pulled into the parking lot stocked with sandwiches and hot coffee for the picketers. Union management called it "unfair labor practices." The picketers, tired of freezing their rumps off in the bitter cold, called it a "might friendly thing to do." The vote went against the union, and things went back to normal—except for the head of the organizing crew, whom the union promptly fired.

"That young feller worked purty hard, even iffen he wuz on the wrong side," Jimmie Joe told his foreman. "See if you cain't give him a job in shipping."

One of the reasons the union had been unsuccessful had to do with the peculiar, for its time, wage program in force in the plant.

"You give em a raise every year when things are good, then they ain't about to give any back when hard times come," Jimmie Joe contended. So he fixed his pay rates at just below the prevailing wage. Then he set up a plan to share plant earnings with the workers in the form of an annual bonus. When things were good, all the workers got a bonus. When they knew things weren't going well, they didn't expect it.

There was no gender differential in the pay scale. And blacks, whom Jimmie Joe never learned to call anything other than "colored people," had the same color-blind opportunity as any other person.

Death came, as it must to all men, to Jimmie Joe Thomas. Though he looked in the pink of health, a massive coronary finished him off at seventy-nine.

He was mourned by his wife, his employees, and the townspeople. In his will, he'd set up a trust that would take care of Sara Jane for the rest of her life. He gave to the usual charities and furnished new uniforms for the local ball team. The balance of his estate went to the workers, in shares proportionate to their years of service in his holdings.

Yes, Jimmie Joe Thomas was a reglar feller—who lived a remarkable life of simple grace.

—*Charles Langley*

When All Is Said

I have a confession to make: a little secret I've been clenching close to me and that I now feel compelled to share.

I read the obituaries. And the newspaper memorials. Every day. Religiously.

"Religiously" is probably the best word for this, because my morning ritual has come to be a sort of religious ritual, one that I can't fully explain but follow anyhow. It's not that I'm looking for people I know in the death notices. I'm still too young and too new to this big city to recognize any of the names of the dead.

I do it anyway, and I don't really know why. In fact, it embarrasses me a little bit, which is why I'll flip the page over if my husband enters the room. I'm not really sure what he'd say if he knew. But in the midst of my family's normal morning mayhem, I am living a separate, parallel life.

Here's how it goes: The newspaper is spread out on the breakfast table. I sip my coffee, take a bite of toast, read an obit, throw some pancakes on the burner for my five-year-old, read another obit, flip the flapjacks and serve, read through another couple of notices, pour the juice for my three kids and yell, "Pack your backpacks," read some more and contemplate life as I slap tuna on whole wheat, stare at photos of smiling faces of the newly dead, wipe peanut butter off the face of my nine-year-old daughter, kiss all good-bye, and sit and contemplate some more.

Weird, I know.

It wasn't always this way. Before this year, I thought of the obituaries as something old people looked at to find out who had been next to pass on.

Then, my dad died. One year ago my father, a remarkable parent, talented doctor, mentor and friend to all, was simply, suddenly gone. The family needed to write a notice for the newspaper and, having no idea what was required, I'd turned to the section that I'd been disparaging all my life. What I found was another world, a more real one, rich with meaning and mystery—a world I suddenly seemed to need.

Dad's death, followed by the catastrophe of the September 11 terrorist attacks on the United States, had unhinged my faith. What used to be simple and sturdy and clear now seemed frighteningly uncertain.

I turned to the obits more and more. Reading this section became a form of morning prayer, a chance to stretch my heart along with my limbs, and a means of coming to terms and reminding myself of what this life is all about.

I suspect my husband would think it morbid or worry that I'm wallowing, when really all I'm doing is trying to figure it out, hoping that maybe, in the little squares of print with their armies of relatives' names, I can find some sort of answer.

Instead, I find comfort. Comfort in company, in the realization that I am not alone, in knowing that all around me people feel this way, too, are also staring into photos, looking up at the sky, crying out to the stars.

You might think it a sad sort of pastime, but it's not. There is much that one can learn from reading the death notices. For one thing, it is impossible to sum up a person's life in a paragraph or two; you have to do a lot of editing. I've noticed no one mentions how incredibly annoying his loved one could be to his younger sister or how he repeatedly "forgot" his homework. Nobody makes note of excessive television watching, messy houses, toothpaste blobs in the sink, or dirty clothes on the floor. The stuff we normally obsess over is filtered out, irrelevant.

Instead, we reflect on what our loved ones loved most in life. We draw bittersweet pictures of them dancing, singing with angels, growing grand tomatoes. We honor the things that make us human: the smiles, the laughter, the love. And we celebrate those who loved life and lived it to the fullest.

In the death notices and memorials, we are surprisingly gracious. We are dignified. We say the words we wished we'd said earlier, imploring others to speak them, too, before it's too late.

Hidden in each small square of print is a fascinating story: There's Penny, daughter of a poultry farmer, who threw grand dinner parties and backpacked across Greece. And Walt, the engineer who learned late in life to dance. We meet quiet Norma, who loved needlework and animals. Pop, whose grandkids still hear him cheering their hockey goals. And cancer-stricken Kate, who loved CNN, chocolate, and Chanel No. 5; who joked just before her death that her children were acting like the KGB; and who realized, after all her family arrived from far and wide, that it was time to go.

Each morning I turn the pages of my newspaper and there it is again—Death—like a slap; I am amazed at its constancy. How could it be, day after day, this relentless wave of names clustered together in the midst of chaos, amidst the busyness of the day's news? I wonder, do they know of each other? Do they lift away together as one, like a flock of gulls alighting from the beach?

One morning, a son's gentle words, "Goodbye, Dad, go with God," surprised a tear from my eye. Another day, it was the simple closing, "And she soars," that snapped my heart. On another, the angry: "Down, down, down into the darkness of the grave . . . I do not approve. And I am not resigned."

My year of obit-reading has not yet resolved my struggles with faith. But it has shown me how I ought to live my life. I have begun a journal for my children and have started volunteering with the old and disadvantaged. I am taking more pictures, giving more hugs, enjoying that extra piece of fudge. I am seeking out those who are silly and sentimental, who bite more from life than they can chew, and who, when they leave this world, will leave it a better place.

My breakfasts with the obits have taught me this: I have a choice. I can walk down a hallway soldier-straight, touching nothing, leaving my path squeaky clean. Or I can be less careful and more passionate, careening off the walls sometimes, leaving smudges of myself as I go. When I reach the end, my marks will still be there.

After all, life is, like the obits, incredibly short.

—Kim Zarzour

The Salvation of
Jan and Kurt

Lucy Hobbs had recently lost her husband and now, in her seventies, found herself living on a Social Security pittance. She could have moved in with her daughter, but she wasn't ready for that yet. Surely, she was still needed somewhere. The advertisement posted on the bulletin board at Stanton's General Store in Alvin, Texas, seemed the perfect answer: "Widower needs housekeeper to cook, clean, and take care of two boys, ten and five years old—room, board, and a small salary."

The door of the ramshackle farmhouse opened, and Mrs. Hobbs introduced herself to a family in a desperate situation. The father, Gus, had lost his wife to cancer in 1943, when Jan Arthur was six years old and Kurt Rolf was only one. A few days before his wife's death, Gus's father, a seaman with Gulf Oil, had been killed when his oil tanker collided with a ship.

Gus's mother had moved in with him and helped care for his boys; but just one year later, she had died of cancer. Shortly after his mother's death, Gus discovered he had colon cancer and subsequently had a colostomy. By the time Lucy Hobbs stepped through their doorway in 1947, Gus had begun to crumble, along with the family finances and the house.

Mrs. Hobbs, gray-haired and grandmotherly plump, peered at Jan and Kurt through round wire-rim glasses that perched on her nose like a small silver bird. The boys were sunburned, bare-chested, and barefoot. From their heads to their toes, they were ragged, skinny, and mosquito-bitten. She knew immediately that she was needed there and took the job.

The unruly boys had driven off every other housekeeper their father had hired. Some left in tears after enduring only one day of Jan's deliberate defiance and disobedience. The boys were often left alone and hungry, subsisting on jelly sandwiches.

The moment Mrs. Hobbs finished moving her few possessions into the drafty farmhouse, Jan began his usual tactics. He pedaled his bike down the driveway and onto the shell road that led to town, several miles from their farm on a busy highway. Mrs. Hobbs lumbered diagonally across the uncut yard, cockleburs and nettles nipping at her ankles, caught his handlebars and told him not to leave the farm.

"You're not my mother, and I don't have to mind

you," Jan spit out angrily.

With surprising strength, she dragged him into the house and plopped him down on a chair. She emphatically told the boys, "I will not put up with any disobedience. If you want homemade biscuits and gravy for dinner, you'd better behave for the rest of the day!" The salvation of Jan and Kurt had begun.

Armed only with the force of her willpower and the promise of regular meals, Mrs. Hobbs brought stability. She began the transformation process by insisting on cleanliness and good manners. "Cleanliness is next to Godliness," she told them. She assigned chores to Jan and Kurt and insisted they do a good job. "Anything worth doing is worth doing well," the boys heard often.

She took them shopping at Stanton's General Store, where they picked out patterned chicken feed sacks, and then she bargained with them, "I'll make shirts for you out of the sacks you pick, but you have to take good care of the chickens." She made sure that the boys fed and watered the chickens, kept the nest boxes filled with clean hay, and gathered the eggs daily. Their rewards were new shirts for school and bacon and eggs for breakfast.

Mrs. Hobbs used Tom Sawyer's tactics to get the boys to plant a garden. "I'd plant it myself, but I want you boys to have some of the fun. And won't you be proud of yourselves when you see those nice straight rows of vegetables sprouting up? And just think how delicious they'll taste." She encouraged them through the preparation and planting, and when the dog days of the project came around, she required they keep the garden weeded and watered. Their reward was a lesson in perseverance and fresh vegetables for dinner: beans, corn, squash, and tomatoes.

She asked them to chop down the weeds in the yard and make a path for her to the clothesline. "I just can't stand thrashing through these weeds to get to the clothesline. I'm afraid I can't do the washing anymore if you boys don't chop me a path." When they complained that they didn't have a lawnmower, she recited one of her favorite principles: "Where there's a will, there's a way," and insisted they do the job with a hoe. Their reward was a yard they could run across without getting stickers in their bare feet and line-dried clothes and linens.

Mrs. Hobbs kept clean sheets on the bed the boys shared. At first, they rebelled at going to sleep at a decent hour, but she insisted, telling them, "Pretend you're going to Mary White's party." Then she tucked them in and made sure they said their prayers. It didn't take long for them to figure out that Mary White's party was a good night's rest between clean white sheets.

The farmhouse was not insulated. It was cooled by fans in the hot Gulf Coast summers, and warmed in the winter by a Dearborn butane space heater located in the kitchen. Tin can lids were tacked over holes in the floor to keep warm air inside and to keep cold wind and mice outside.

During the intensely hot summer afternoons, Mrs. Hobbs called the boys into the house. "You boys come in here and rest a while before that sun turns you into lobsters." At first they rebelled, but they soon enjoyed resting and listening to the radio: the King of Swing, Bob Wills and the Light Crust Dough-boys from Burris Mills, out of Fort Worth.

On frigid winter mornings, Mrs. Hobbs lit the Dearborn and started breakfast before she woke the boys. Drawn by the smell of bacon frying, they shivered all the way to the kitchen, the only warm room in the house, where they dressed for school.

Lucy Hobbs was not opposed to using dessert as an incentive to good manners, hard work, and compliance with her rules. When they had accomplished a particularly obnoxious task, such as cleaning out the pigpen or chopping weeds with the hoe, she would treat them to homemade donuts rolled in sugar or their favorite, rice pudding.

With the structure of regular meals and bedtimes, Jan and Kurt began to blossom. They were occasionally tempted to defy Mrs. Hobbs and go skinny-dipping in snake-ridden rice canals, but drawn by the delicious smell of fried chicken and mashed potatoes and gravy wafting through the kitchen window, they resisted the urge to run away.

The boys' father continued his downward spiral, drinking more and more heavily, coming home less and less. Mrs. Hobbs and the boys were often stuck in the country, miles from town, with no transportation. Gus was no longer able to pay her, but Mrs. Hobbs stayed on, using her Social Security check to buy butane and food. She was petrified at what would happen to Jan and Kurt if she left. When they told her they were afraid she would leave, she reassured them: "God gave me a mission to save you boys, and I'm going to stay as long as I can."

But after five years with them, her health and eyesight began to fail. In spite of her fears, she couldn't keep up with the job of raising them. Mrs. Hobbs told them many times that she would have to leave soon. At first Jan and Kurt panicked and begged her to stay. But after having heard her expressing her need to leave over and over, they no longer took it seriously. One day while the boys were at school, she packed everything she owned into one suitcase and went to live with her daughter in Galveston. Now in her eighties, she had given all she had to give.

Several years later, her daughter brought her to Alvin to see Jan and Kurt. She was growing deaf and nearly blind. They were happy to see her, but as teenage boys, they were not adept at expressing tender emotions. She never told them she loved them, but she did. They never told her they loved her, but they did.

Lucy Hobbs could not have realized how well she had accomplished her mission. Her lessons had soaked into their souls, and they grew like oak trees, strong and beautiful. I have benefited from her sacrifices. I married Jan.

On a frosty December dawn, I flick a switch and the house begins to warm; another switch, and the coffee perks. I sit at the kitchen table and watch the outline of bare oak branches appear as the first gray strokes of light brush across the black sky. My prayer for the soul of Lucy Hobbs rises with the steam from my coffee. If she were here today I would tell her about a family that she never knew belonged to her. I would spread before her a meal of her own making: the meat and potatoes of our lives—a marriage of more than forty years, four children, and eight grandchildren. I would see to her comfort, cover her shoulders with a warm shawl, keep her coffee cup filled to the brim. And at last, reward her with the rice pudding of words not said to her in time: They love you. You are the mother they remember.

—*Nancy Gustafson*

Power Ball of Love

Every summer, I go back to the beach where I almost drowned thirty years ago. I look at the blue-green waters of the Gulf of Mexico that would have taken me far out toward the horizon had it not been for my stepsister. At ten years old, she walked chest deep into the crashing, frothy water and yanked me from the riptide. Five years separated our ages and different mothers separated us genetically, but that day we became sisters of the soul as we sat sputtering and coughing on the sandy white shores of the Gulf.

Two years later, she saved my younger brother from drowning, too. Only he was thrown headfirst into the swimming pool by our father, who was so inebriated he could hardly stand up.

"Let him learn like I did," he had slurred as he threw his three-year-old son into the pool, while his daughters watched, petrified, from the far corner of the yard.

Our brother was afraid of water and never went near it. His tiny body flailed; we were frozen with fear. *I'm going to stand here and watch my brother drown*, I'd thought to myself, as I gripped the cool metal of the swing set.

Finally my stepsister moved, although at the time I thought it was more from training than anything else. Our brother was her responsibility; born late in my mother's life, he was an unwanted child and so his care was thrust upon another unwanted child, the stepchild. I was the middle sibling, the firstborn to my mother, and never sure what my status was in the "wanted" category.

My sister ran to the pool and jumped in, fully clothed. She dragged the boy to the side and pushed him up onto the hot cement. Our father laughed and stumbled back indoors.

We never spoke of the incident.

Later that summer, she taught my brother how to swim. Gently calming his fear that had now grown to near hysteria, she trickled water down his back and shoulders while he sat on the side of the pool near the shallow end, only his feet immersed. I would watch from the deep end as she cooed and coaxed him little by little to her hip, then to arm's length, while he kicked. By some slowly unfolding miracle,

I watched as he dunked his head under for the first time, late that summer, and she and I yelled and clapped and slapped the water at his victory as he beamed at us with water dripping into his eyes.

I have often wondered if either of my parents ever said to her, "Thanks for saving first my daughter and now my son from drowning."

It is not easy for any child to grow up in a home where one parent is an alcoholic and the other parent is too wrapped up in the alcoholic to tend to the infinite needs of growing children. It is even harder for a stepchild, a child who is thrust into the home by the marriage of the adults.

I was four years old when I learned, through one of my parents' fights, that my sister and I did not share the same mother. For years I thought she was adopted, until I discovered who the mystery gift-giver at Christmas was, and it wasn't Santa Claus. My stepsister's mother always sent things we could never use, like thick heavy stockings, even though we lived in Florida. My mother would tuck away the gifts, still in their boxes, on a high shelf of the hall closet.

Both of us were incredibly resilient. One of our favorite things to do was to roll white bread into what we called "power balls," pretending that when we ate them we assumed superhuman abilities. We flew boldly through the air, from one twin bed to the other, jumping like maniacs across the room with towels on our backs to represent capes. We invented our own world with those power balls. It was a world that could be created only by two children who were already wounded and world-weary. Finally, our mother would holler that we were going to break the springs in the mattresses or our father would wonder out loud where the loaf of bread had gone, and our game would come to an abrupt end. But those power balls had already bound us together. It was a game we played religiously until she moved out.

She left home when I was thirteen, after the millionth bitter argument with my mother. There were no good-byes or farewells. I came home from school one day to find an empty closet and an empty bureau. I did not even know where she had gone. My parents were angry and secretive about it. Conversations in loud whispers ended abruptly whenever my brother or I entered the room. I heard rumors about myself and my family at high school, about what happened that day to cause my stepsister to leave with no job and no place to live. She still had a semester of high school to complete. I cried myself to sleep every night until I learned she was living with a friend on the beach, those blue-green waters of the Gulf washing the sand clean just beyond the door to her house.

The next time I saw her, we built a sand castle together outside that door. It was three years after she left.

She came to pick me up in a noisy red Volkswagen with a dog named Faith hanging out of the side window. She had gotten the dog at the pound, she'd said, on the day they were going to have her put to sleep. Faith stepped on my thighs and licked my face, while my sister drove me across the bridge and onto the slender finger of land where she lived. She had called my mother and said she wanted to see me, that she missed me, and that she was coming to get me. But I didn't know this at the time. All I knew was that I could have collapsed with relief and something else I could not name when she pulled up into the driveway, her long straight hair held back with a baseball cap, her face wearing a smile that said, "I'm mostly okay."

Soon after that visit, she moved to California. She lived on a houseboat, which I thought sounded fabulously romantic. I overlooked my mother's derisive comments about it, about how it meant she didn't have any money and couldn't hold down a job. Whenever I got a letter from her letting me know she was alive, that same feeling of relief poured over me. I spent long hours imagining her life on the houseboat, her view of the mountains, the water rocking her to sleep every night.

After I left for college, our correspondence fell off a bit, but we kept at it. She got married on the West Coast when I was a freshman. Because the wedding was held during my final exams, I could not attend. Our parents refused to attend. A few weeks later, I received a picture of my stepsister in a flowing white gown, her hair bundled and surrounded by flowers on top of her head, standing beside a tall man with dark eyes gazing serenely into the camera. By the time I met him, they had had their first child.

They were married almost five years when I got a letter saying that they were coming through Atlanta, where I was then living. Did I want to see her, meet her family? We hadn't seen each other in over six years. I was working full time as a counselor at a drug addiction center, trying, I suppose, to work out some of my own issues about my father's alcoholism.

I pulled the wedding picture from my purse and stared at it, trying to reconcile the beautiful smiling bride with the skinny frightened kid I had grown up with. What happened to her sorrow, I wondered, and the shame she had always been made to feel because she was the stepchild? Where, beyond the smile that beamed from her face, had she tucked them?

I wondered what she thought of me when she looked at the picture I had sent her in my reply. Did she wonder what I had done with my sorrow, too?

She came to my home on a hot July day, holding a tiny baby in her arms. Her husband stood behind her, one hand protectively on her shoulder. When I opened the door, my body rigid with tension and anticipation, time collapsed. I laughed, this time with tears in my eyes. She laughed, too. We hugged, squishing the baby between us. We were who we had always been together.

We didn't talk about the past that day. I held her son and rocked him when he cried. He looked amazingly like our younger brother. Her husband smiled at me over his coffee cup with liquid brown eyes. I wondered how much she had told him about our family.

Ten years passed before we saw each other again. I guess people get busy with their own lives. We talked a few times on the phone, but the conversations were awkward and stilted because we weren't asking each other what we really wanted to ask: "What was it like for you?"

Finally, after years of therapy and coming to terms with my father's alcoholism, I talked to my sister one beautiful spring day when she was visiting her husband's relatives in a town close enough for me to drive to. We sat outside under pink dogwood trees in full bloom. The air had that crisp, just-washed smell to it. We watched her three children play in the backyard. I decided to take the plunge. I took a deep breath and asked her what it had been like for her to grow up in such a punishing atmosphere, where she had been scapegoated in every sense of the word.

"I've forgiven them," she said.

"You what?" I asked after I picked my jaw up off the ground. Forgiveness had always been a biggie for me, a skill I had never mastered where my parents were concerned.

"I've forgiven them," she repeated. "You can't go on hating a person for being who they are. Our parents, all three of them, were products of their environments. They didn't know any better."

I was stunned into silence and mentally filed away the words, so I could bring them out and examine them another time.

Two years later, her husband died after a brief battle with a rare disease. He was forty-five years old; my stepsister, forty-three. Their youngest child was five, about to begin school. I could not attend the funeral because no planes were flying. It was four days after September 11, 2001.

I've often wondered how much pain a person can be expected to be dealt in a lifetime. My stepsister said she had forgiven our parents for how they'd raised us. I read once that forgiving one's parents is giving up all hope of having had a better childhood. Perhaps, in order for my sister to have hope for the future, she had to give up hope about the past.

We rarely see each other now. We live in different states and lead totally different lives. But we write, and I think of her often, especially of those fateful days when she literally saved both my life and the life of my brother. I think about her forgiving our parents for being highly imperfect people. I think what it must be like to completely forgive someone who has harmed you in ways you may not even realize, to offer up the anguish and sorrow of a child to something higher than yourself, and to feel that anguish transformed and sent back to you as something you can live with: acceptance, perhaps, and inner peace. And I wonder what it would be like to save the lives of two children and never hear anyone say thank-you.

My stepsister has taught me that no matter how crummy the hand of cards that you are dealt is, there is always room in the heart for hope and love. I understand now that forgiveness is a gift you give yourself, and that by forgiving our parents, my stepsister had salvaged her own life.

And by teaching me this lesson, she saved mine again.

—*Kelly L. Stone*

Stopping Traffic

This is a story about my best friend. Actually, it's not just about my best friend; it's also about my husband, who happens to be the same person. But that's beside the point.

Perhaps I also ought to mention that this is only one of many amazing stories I tell about him, because he is, in truth, an amazing person. But that, too, is beside the point.

Here is the point: This is a heartwarming story about an amazing man. And it goes like this:

One blustery, wintry day, at around 4:00 in the afternoon, my friend and I were driving peacefully along in the right lane of the Garden State Parkway in New Jersey. The Garden State Parkway at some points has five lanes of speeding traffic. During almost any season, most of the cars are heading madly toward the New Jersey shore in the misguided hope that they will find peace and quiet at the water's edge. Somewhere in my soul I am convinced that if they would drive less madly on the way to serenity, they would find it sooner. But I digress.

On this particular day, at this particular hour, we noticed that the traffic was developing a very peculiar pattern. It was racing along in the second, fourth, and fifth lanes, but the right and middle lanes were considerably slower. Perplexed, we moved to the second lane and prayed it was not an accident (which could keep us there for hours). Construction was the roadblock of choice.

Pretty soon we noticed a car pulled over on the shoulder. Standing near it was a rather attractive girl of perhaps twenty-five or so, frantically waving her hands. And there, in the right lane, was something fairly large, which we figured was screwing up traffic. We pulled over to where the girl was parked and got out of our car. She was practically in tears, but didn't have to tell us that the article in the right lane was a mattress or that a box spring was in the third lane of traffic, getting hit occasionally by cars.

Still holding back tears, she explained that she'd just bought the set, which had been tied on top of the car by the salesperson. But the wind had knocked them off her car and onto the parkway. Panicked, she'd pulled over and had been trying to get someone to help her. She didn't have a cell phone, and, when you really need them, police cars stay away in droves. So she'd been standing there in the bitter cold with her hands up for almost fifteen minutes.

She was there for almost fifteen minutes, and nobody—nobody—had stopped. Until us.

Where are the good Samaritans of this world? Where are those caring Americans who help each other out in a pinch? If this had been a car accident, at least one other car would have stopped.

Never mind. You need only one, and we were it.

We listened to her story sympathetically. Then, without any hesitation, my friend stepped out into the highway and stopped traffic.

I swear. He put up his hand and walked across the highway, stopping traffic. Stopping speeding cars swerving to avoid an annoying obstacle. Stopping cars hell-bent on getting to a peaceful spot. Never thinking they might swerve into him. Fearlessly he stepped to the third lane and pulled the damaged box spring over to the side of the road. He then walked to lane one and saved the mattress. Then he waved the traffic on.

He waved the traffic on.

The girl was dumbstruck. I was frozen to the spot. My friend was not at all disturbed. In fact, he didn't notice our concern at all. There was more to be done. He had to figure out how to tie the mattress set back on the car safely.

Impossible. Her car was too small to start with, which is probably why she got into this predicament. So our car, which was a sight larger, would substitute. But how? Never mind how to tie it. First we had to get it up there. Two frail women (I am five feet, two inches and not very strong) and a sixty-four-year-old man (did I mention we are in our sixties?) would have to hoist first the box spring and then the mattress up on our car.

That was the plan: She and I would take one end, and he would take the other. Easily said if you've never lifted a queen-size box spring and mattress in a gusty February wind, on a highway with speeding cars, to the top of a car that's taller than you.

The first mishap was me. I tripped and dropped my end and fell onto my knee, which immediately started gushing blood all over her box spring. Great. And the scar will be there forever.

Tying a handkerchief around my throbbing knee, we began again. This time successfully.

Resting for a moment before hoisting the mattress on top of the box spring, my friend advised the girl, who was still terribly upset, that she would, of course, get her money back or a new set in exchange, because the salesperson was at fault, not she. We suggested driving back to the store with the set, but when we called on our cell phone, the store was closed. The problem of returning it would be hers or theirs. If she did not get satisfaction, she could call us, and we would help. My friend is, after all, a lawyer. No, no, no. Not *that* kind of lawyer. He is an intellectual property lawyer. You know, the kind that deals with copyrights and trademarks. Again, I digress.

Not without further difficulty, we succeeded in hoisting the mattress on top of the box spring. Now we had to secure them. My friend's plan was to utilize whatever we had at hand. This included the torn string that was left from the original tie-up, some bungees we had in our car, a few T-shirts that he knotted together, and God knows what else. To make sure of no further mishap, he and the girl would sit in the front seats with the windows open, holding onto the set as he drove, very slowly. I would drive her car, following them to her house, which was a few miles away.

Oh, yes. Just as we were ready to leave, the highway authority drove up. A nice man, but a little too late. He did help us get safely back on the highway, though, and assured us that we could drive slowly.

When we arrived at the girl's home, she jumped out of the car, ran over to me, and gave me a big hug. It seems that while driving, she and my friend exchanged bits of information. She had once been a dancer. So had I, when I was young. She presently worked for a legal magazine that my friend subscribes to. And she had been a secretary at a law firm that my friend knew quite well. Small world.

Before parting we shared once more the unbelievable horror of her plight and received a hundred tearful thank-yous and hugs. We promised to keep in touch.

A final digression . . .

I often wonder. If that girl on the side of the road had been a white girl, would someone have stopped to help her sooner? I forgot to mention: she is black; we are not. I know how she must feel. I was looking for a cab in New York City not two months before on a snowy, frigid night. I had on black gloves, a black scarf around my face to help keep out the cold, and a black hat. Not one cab stopped for me, though a number of them were looking for fares. Finally, a black cabbie pulled over, and as I got in, I removed the scarf from my face. He looked at me confused. I was white! He could not understand why all those other cabs hadn't stopped for me. Couldn't he see that for a moment, at least, I was black?

My story has a happy ending. Our new friend was given a new mattress set with apologies from the store.

Would you like to hear about the time my husband saved a forest from a catastrophic fire? Single-handedly he braved the elements, fighting the persistent flames with just the shirt off his back, and got a terrible case of poison ivy, which lasted all summer.

He was only a little younger then.

—Gila Zalon

Prince of Paupers

His mother named him, in the best boy-named-Sue tradition, Laverne Elmer. *Elmer* for his father. *Laverne*, maybe, to dress up the plain last name of Jones.

It must have caused him some hassles when he was a kid. As an adult, he called himself Verne, but once confessed the Laverne to me. Why, I don't know, because I tended to tweak him about it. Maybe he liked the tweaking. One thing is certain, I never knew about the Elmer. Not until he died January 12, 2002.

People who worked for him called him Mr. Jones, not because they were required to, but because it fit. The captain of his own ship, he was the administrator of old Edgefield Manor, a hulking brick building housing more than 300 troubled old souls, anchored in a backwater between the small Oregon towns of Wood Village and Troutdale. First a poor farm, later a nursing home, it is now known as McMenamins Edgefield, a stylish retreat of soft beds, fluffy bathrobes, and designer beer.

The fact that his Edgefield ended up with its own brewery, winery, and distillery amuses Verne, a staunch teetotaling Baptist and caregiver to aged, but determined alcoholics.

Those drinkers still ambulatory at Edgefield Manor would go AWOL now and then, winding up immobilized in one of Troutdale's taverns. Verne would get a phone call in the late evening at the administrator's house at Edgefield (he lived next to the shop, so to speak) and go out in the night to round up the stray. Once, an artist painted two landscapes of Edgefield in gratitude for being fetched home.

And Edgefield was home. Jones, his wife, and the staff were parents to a family with no other place to go. Some were true paupers, institutionalized leftovers from the poor-farm days. Others were damaged souls who found shelter and fine care when the county made Edgefield a top-notch nursing home.

Jones started working there when the poor farm was still a farm and its residents labored in the fields in exchange for bread and board. When the county quit the place in 1982, he closed its doors and retired, choosing to go down with his ship.

The last ten years were painful. In 1972, without

warning or even basic courtesy, the county chairman announced his intention to quit pouring money into the aging buildings and to send its residents elsewhere. Those who called the old brick manor home read it first in the newspaper and went into shock. Jones was called from his house next door. The pain in the place was palpable, and he spread himself thin, like salve. He was, I think, a true public servant.

He had no illusions about those in his care. He knew that "the flasher" would expose himself to women at every opportunity. He knew well the rage expended in the drying-out room, where alcoholics ended their benders. He was charmed by the lady who put on her hat, climbed on the bus, and went dancing in Portland every few days. And he laughed unofficially when tanned and handsome Lucky, who sat by the road in his wheelchair, sneaked a woman into his room.

The place was an odd repository for the remnants of shattered dreams—straitjackets, size 52 men's green plaid shorts, battered billiard tables, leftover wooden legs, carpet bags from 1922, and a pair of ladies' dancing shoes, size 10, in gold.

In the last decade he saw it all sorted out, watched the patients and the employees leave one by one. And on that last day, he walked with me through the empty building, closing doors, checking boxes, and finally climbing to the top floor to ring the bell that had once summoned workers from the fields.

The next day the bell was stolen, and Edgefield began, as he said, to go to pot. Later, he stood on a decaying balcony unable to believe that the McMenamin brothers could fix up the place. And on the night the old lodge first opened its doors to guests, he and his wife were there as first-nighters. He took his key but came right back, apologizing that he needed another room. He'd been assigned the former "rubber room," the drunk room, he said, and could not stay there. Too many demons, he explained.

I suspect Laverne Elmer Jones of true compassion—the kind that lets you see demons, even though they are not your own.

—*Sharon Nesbit*

This story was first published in *The Gresham Outlook*, January 29, 2002.

So I Ask You

I have given up remembering hotel names, calling them what they were two buyouts ago. But a good friend of my brother's has died, and my brother needs to come "home" for the funeral. He also needs a place to stay that is not designed for the rich and famous.

A directory assistance operator helps me, laughing when I say I'm in Easton but can't remember the two local hotel names. I don't say that I can't read signs or the phone book.

I call the two hotels, promising myself I'll remember their names, knowing I won't. I begin to wonder what else there might be in Bethlehem or Phillipsburg—partly because I want to be thorough but also because I just want to know. I decide not to embarrass myself again with directory assistance. So I ask you.

You happily look up names and numbers in the area, telling me you wanted something useful to do.

We've had these discussions before. It isn't just hotels. It's also banks and drugstores. And, "What office complex did they move to?" And while we're at it, "How do I get there?"

My brother always says I'm hopeless at giving directions. So I ask you. You drove for years and loved it. When your health worsened, you got a power wheelchair and cruised as far as it would go.

It used to be, when I wanted to know what things looked like and how much they cost, I asked you. After a while, I didn't have to ask. You knew what I liked. You've often said I have no willpower when I shop with a good-sighted narrator. It's true, though I hate to admit it.

You love the adventure. "Have you ever seen bagpipes? . . . No? Well, come on. I'm sure he'll show them to us." Or, "Have you ever seen a holly bush?" as we're walking by a large specimen.

I have handled fencing swords, teddy bears made of real fur, and blown-glass earrings. I've asked you and have touched suits of armor, Queen Elizabeth the First's Renaissance fair costume, seashell wind chimes, and more lace than you can shake ten white canes at. I've played a harpsichord, I know how tall conga drums are, and I've hefted some really big handbells.

You bring things back from longer travels for me to touch. You hand me a part of a plant. I can't guess what it is, so I ask you.

"Raw cotton," you tell me.

I am surprised by it, having never thought about what it would look like. I am amazed that you would think enough to bring some back for me, wondering how you would have explained taking a piece of a cotton plant for a blind friend in Pennsylvania. Luckily, no one stops to ask what you are doing.

Normally, I would never ask so many questions, because questions call attention to how much I don't know or can't do. But it's really helpful to have some people whom I can ask anything. So I ask you:

"How far can you see in a straight line?"

"What can you see from this height on your balcony?"

"How do I look in this outfit?"

"Are you sure birds have only two feet?"

I have never had sight, and my impression was that birds must have four feet because they walk on the ground like other animals. If you think that's weird, consider what I thought bears looked like, given that the only bears I could touch were teddy bears.

Your new view from the chair allows you to travel more slowly; to see things that people standing or in cars would not see.

When I am walking behind you and holding the

chair handles, it also allows for some strange looks from nearby people. After all, it appears that I am pushing and steering the chair. If I carry my white cane unfolded, we can part a large crowd this way. I confess to enjoying the deception, knowing you are controlling where we go.

I sometimes want to know about the looks and actions we are causing. So I ask you. I suspect that we are both a little too gleeful about the game, but you always tell me the best reactions.

My absolute favorite exploration was something I didn't have to ask you.

We were cruising past the construction at Easton's Bachmann Tavern. You noticed the stars carved into the wooden steps. (I believe that people who find stars in their lives are particularly spiritual.) You wheeled me over to feel the shapes. We decided that the holes were cut to allow the wood to dry, a space for water to evaporate. No one standing would have seen the stars.

I don't know why the star shapes were cut. Maybe for good luck? I don't know if they're still there. Perhaps you and I will chat. And I'll ask you.

—*Nancy Scott*

The Dollar Dance

With his mom on one side and his dad on the other, Nathan made his way proudly toward the front of the church. Fifteen years had passed since Nate, then only seven, had prayed for his divorced parents to reconcile. Now, for this one special moment in time, his prayer had been answered, as his parents escorted him down the aisle on his wedding day.

His face flushed with excitement and summer heat. A small-town Wisconsin boy decked out in his first tuxedo, he looked uncomfortable and out of his element. His bride-to-be, Kady, waited in front of the altar, a beatific smile lighting her face when she caught Nate's eyes.

"That boy is no candidate for Harvard," Nate's Grammy Lorraine had said more than once over the years. Nate was all boy, physically strong and competitive. But during his birth, twenty-two years earlier, he had lingered too long in the birth canal before entering this world by cesarean section. We knew the prognosis was not good when the doctor reported "lack of oxygen to the brain," but we quietly hoped he might miraculously "grow out of it," like some kids outgrow childhood allergies or a lisp.

By the time Nate entered second grade, his teachers were sending home notes encouraging his parents to have him tested and placed in an appropriate "alternative" educational program. They resisted, insisting that their son had a right to be in the "mainstream" with his friends and with Tiffany, his older sister. Tiffany was not only Nate's sister; she was also his rock, his greatest supporter, and his biggest fan. As Nate's aunt, I, too, was aware of my nephew's "limitations" and fiercely protective of him.

My brother, Nate's dad, proved no match for the stress of raising a "challenged" son and gave in to the persuasion of Tanqueray gin sometime during Nate's preschool days. Before Nate was seven, their mom was single, working hard to keep the family sheltered and fed, and he and Tiffany were latchkey kids. My brother drifted from tavern to tavern, and in and out of consciousness, as he lost his business, his self-esteem, and the respect of his family.

When the family gathered for holidays, the cousins whispered jokes and giggled about Nate's "condition."

"Hey, Nate, let's play Pictionary." And then they'd wait with anticipation at Nate's turn for him to get a word they were certain he could not read, ready for his disability to provide their entertainment. Because Nate always accepted their invitations and laughed easily at his mistakes, he became a popular pick as teammate. His easygoing example took the stress from the otherwise competitive game-playing, and Nate became a catalyst for lightheartedness.

We adults avoided talking about Nate's limitations, afraid of hurting his parents' feelings, afraid that discussing what the boy lacked would somehow intensify his mental shortcomings.

Two family myths stood in the way of a more compassionate and proactive approach to Nate's "differences." One, an adage that Nate's grandmother often cited, had stuck through the generations: "Never trouble trouble till trouble troubles you; it only doubles trouble and troubles others too." When I go through old photos of family gatherings, I imagine that the caption on the group shots should read, "Maybe if we don't talk about 'it,' 'it' will disappear."

The second myth: Education, especially college, is the only road to happiness and fulfillment in life. My mother's older brother and sister both taught school during the Great Depression. Uncle Lawrence, the most distinguished of the two, taught at a prestigious boys' academy in Missouri. We listened to grand stories and gazed in awe at the large portrait of Headmaster Lawrence in his starched collar and black string tie. He glared down at us from his perch on the dining room wall, a proper teacher's scowl on his face. In our family we were pointed down a path that led to academic accomplishment. When viewed through the lens of Myth Number Two, Nathan's condition seemed even more hopeless. Our fear of his impending failure and our social embarrassment kept us paralyzed.

Oblivious to our suffering on his account, Nate was a relaxed and happy child. He threw himself into family festivities. He idolized his older cousin, James, who returned Nate's adoration with taunts. James was woefully bereft of praise from boys his own age, so he not only tolerated, but actively sought out, the hero worship of his younger, mentally challenged cousin. James enjoyed having someone he could treat with derision, on whom he could play practical jokes without jeopardizing his "idol" status. Every despot hopes for such a subject. Other cousins counseled Nate, "James is too old for you, Nate. Besides, he isn't very nice to you. Why don't you stay and play with us?" But what Nate lacked in I.Q., he made up for in devotion to his "cool" cousin, James, as well as tender forgiveness for slights.

As Nate grew, it became even more apparent that he was not like the rest. After he was diagnosed with attention deficit hyperactivity disorder as well as learning disabilities, his teachers recommended medication. Finally, to keep him from being removed from class for "behavioral problems," his mother agreed to put Nate on Ritalin to keep him "focused" on his schoolwork and less intent on entertaining his classmates. He sure could keep them laughing!

His behavior did improve when he was medicated, but he also lost his appetite and sense of humor, and he was too depressed and lethargic to play on the basketball team. When the family gathered, we complimented Nate on his "good" behavior. During his junior year of high school, unbeknownst to his doctor and his mother, Nate stopped taking his medication. He told me several years later that he did not "feel like himself" when he took the drug. He realized that if he just acted subdued and kept quiet in school, he could stop taking the pills and no one would notice. No one did.

Kady Lovelace met Nathan when he was a senior in high school and she was a junior attending a rival school. She was named valedictorian of her class. When she and Nathan came to visit us the summer after she graduated, I took her aside to give her our story—the "family truth" about her fiancé, Nathan. I felt it was my responsibility to warn her. After all, members of our family were all either bound for college or college graduates, so, of course, we knew what was best for our grandson, our nephew, our cousin, our Nathan.

She listened politely and said, "Thanks, Peg, I know all about Nate's learning disabilities." She leaned over the table toward me. "I enjoy doing our finances. Math was my best subject. My mom and grandma love Nate as much as I do. They say his heart is true, and that's all a man needs to succeed in life." Kady smiled down at the ring sparkling on her left hand as she finished, "We're saving up for our wedding next year. And we hope you and Uncle Doug will be there to celebrate our day."

We were. And what a day it was! We were all invited to be a part of the ceremony. Uncle Doug and Cousin Colin were ushers; Aunt Julia and I read passages from the Bible. After dinner, while I watched Tiffany help cut the cake, a curious expression came over her face—a look of admiration, love, and triumph all mixed together. In that moment I was able to put away the tired old family story of what Nathan "wouldn't" or "couldn't" have, of what he would miss because of his limitations. Filled by my revelation, I understood that my nephew was writing his own life story, an original story, not based on tired family myths.

Nathan is God's gift to our family. He models and will continue to teach us every day of his life the lessons we most need to learn: to live in the moment, to believe all things are possible, to love unconditionally, and to hope always for the best.

The best man announced that he was collecting for the dollar dance. The women hurried to the dance floor with dollar bills clenched in their hands, waiting for their turn to dance with the groom. I stood at the head of the line. Nate stepped forward and asked for our attention.

"I hope you will excuse me. I can't memorize, so I will have to read this to you." He reached into his tux pocket and brought out a tiny, wrinkled scrap of paper. "I am truly blessed to have Kady as my wife, because she always helps me do my best. She is my best friend. She even took me to dance lessons, so I wouldn't step on your toes." He folded up the paper and reached for my hand. "Come on, Aunt Peg, let's dance."

—Peggy MacKay

Give Your Heart Away

"Don't give your heart away, Michelle." I could hear my mother's words, almost as if her voice were echoing down the sterile hallway that was silent except for the occasional clang of metal crib sides being lowered and raised.

I held the child in my arms and briefly wondered how I had gotten myself into this situation. Pictures on the evening news had led me to volunteer in the Casa de Copii St. Maria Home for Children, deep in the heart of Iaşi, Romania. Even though eight years had passed since the fall of the communist rule, in 1989, the scars were still evident in Iaşi. Bullet holes marked the walls of buildings, suspicion continued to shroud the faces of the people accustomed to living in fear, and hurt grew behind the blank stares of the orphanage children.

Romania had once been a rich, vibrant country,

known as the breadbasket of Eastern Europe. The city of Iaşi was now reduced to dark, dirty streets and dusty patches of hard-packed clay where lawns and green should have been. Tall concrete apartments and crumbling cement buildings blocked the view of the sun. Abandoned dogs roamed free to scavenge what scraps they could find, as did the street children who had escaped the orphanage system. Broken men and veiled, sad-eyed women clutching babies begged for coins at the sides of the roads. The sidewalks were congested with people and parked cars, and the streets were crammed with fast-moving vehicles.

All that my friend, Jennifer, and I wanted to do was to help the neglected children who were warehoused in the city's overcrowded and underfunded orphanages. We were not even sure what that "help" would be like, but in the Casa de Copii St. Maria, a home for infants up to age two, our aid would simply take the form of cuddling and playing.

When we first stepped off the dusty front yard into the Casa, the sticky June heat turned oppressive as we entered the stifling and muggy orphanage, whose screenless windows were closed to prevent the ţanţars (mosquitoes) from entering. The wide and empty hallways were lined on one side with closed doors that hid the rooms that held the children. The air stank of sour milk, musty laundry, and stale urine. The feeling that something was wrong nagged at me, but I pushed the thought away.

Uneasily, we climbed the stairs to the second floor, which housed the older babies, and pushed open a heavy door. Through the widening crack, row after row of rusted, chipped, white metal cribs were revealed. The acrid smell of urine and vomit swelled in our nostrils, and it was easy to see that the battered, thin crib mattresses were damp and covered with stains. Tiny dark eyes stared back at us; not one child smiled. One little girl rocked her head back and forth, back and forth. Another child moved to the end of her crib and watched me intently.

I smiled tentatively. "*Buna*," I said softly. Hello. At that one word, the walls crumbled down, and she smiled and held out her arms for me to hold her. I lifted the little girl out of her iron prison, momentarily repulsed by the wet pee stain that ran up her back, and then cuddled her close.

Babies suddenly clamored at Jenn and me, and I put my arm around another child. Crina, the little girl who rocked, stopped her movements as I put my hand on her face, but as soon as I took it away, her little mind shut down again and she returned to her rocking. I motioned for Jenn to hold her, and we began to sing and play with the little ones. The babies bounced and babbled and reached to be picked up, until the nurses walked in to see what was going on.

It was then that I realized what was wrong when

we had first walked through the doors: the silence. The building housed more than 200 infants and toddlers, yet there was not a sound. I later discovered that the babies were afraid to cry; the overworked staff would scream at them to be quiet. The babies shrank back in silence when the nurses entered.

I was sitting beside an empty crib, holding a boy named Gheorghe. If ever a baby looked like a stockbroker, it was the serious, round-faced Gheorghe. A nurse carrying a baby by one arm stormed in and dumped the child in the crib beside me. Grabbing the little girl by the ankle, the nurse jerked her closer and ripped off the rough cotton diaper the child was wearing and proceeded to wrap her in a new one. I glimpsed the child's bottom, which was so raw it bled. Not once through this rough process did the little girl even whimper. The nurse cast me a disdainful look and left.

Gheorghe was returned to his crib with a promise of more cuddles later, and I picked up the little girl. She did not cry, did not smile, did not cuddle up against me. Mihaiela remained stiff and rigid, her eyes vacant. As I gazed at this child, her blank eyes staring off into the distance, my mother's words floated through my head.

"Don't give your heart away, Michelle!"

Oh, she'd meant well. She knew that I poured my heart out to hurting things and was often wounded in the process. She knew that it would tear my heart apart if I allowed myself to get attached to these children and then had to leave them behind. She cautioned me to only play with and cuddle them, and not to fall in love with them.

But wasn't that why I was here? Wasn't I here because no one loved these children? Could I live with myself if I just played and cuddled with Mihaiela, but continued to deprive this child of the love she so desperately craved but had no hope for?

I looked down at Mihaiela, who continued to stare vacantly off to the side, and in an instant I made my decision.

"I'm not going to let you, little girl," I whispered fiercely. "I am not going to let you give up on life. I am not going to let you die if I can help it." And at that moment, I loved her.

Every day when we arrived at the orphanage, I would go to Mihaiela's crib and cuddle her. I would tote her with me as I played with the other children. The first two days she remained stiff; no one was home in her body. But on the third day, I felt the little muscles relax, and she cuddled her body against me. By the end of the week, she was blowing raspberries into my neck and reaching for toys. The ultimate triumph came when I put her down one night and she started to cry. . . . She felt safe enough to cry. I patted her back until she fell asleep and then crept back to our apartment, elated! "My" little girl was metamorphosing into a rosy-cheeked, fuzzy-haired sweetheart with an engaging, goofy little grin.

My heart was wrapped around this little girl's baby fingers, and I was on a mission. Mihaiela had a twisted, club foot, and I had been told that in Romania that would destine her for the Casa de Handicapat, a horrific place where she would be warehoused until she died. Having pulled her from the brink once, I could not let her return to it when her condition was so easily correctible.

In my limited Romanian, I badgered and pushed, prayed and asked and begged, until finally one of the doctors in the orphanage agreed to arrange for Mihaiela and I to meet with an orthopedic surgeon. At the hospital, my translator gasped in shock as she realized we were meeting with the top surgeon in the country. A surgeon who was far above the grasp of an abandoned child had agreed to stoop to the bottom of the social gutter. After trying to discourage me from assisting this child and advising me to pick a more acceptable baby to help instead, he sighed at my determination and agreed to perform the surgery the following week. He also outlined other procedures that Mihaiela would need in order to correct hidden orthopedic and cardiac concerns.

By then, with a sinking heart, I had to go home. Another mission worker agreed to watch out for

Mihaiela and to ensure that she received the surgery to correct her club foot. I promised to raise the necessary funds to pay for the additional surgeries. I gave the little girl a final kiss and laid her back in her crib. Then I turned my back and walked away.

It broke my heart. What good had I really done? Would being loved and abandoned again be worse than never having been loved at all? What would she think when I didn't come back? Would she wait for me, day after day, and then begin to slide back into her vacant stare, willing herself to die?

My mother greeted me at the airport gate, the look on her face warm but worried.

"You gave your heart away, didn't you?" she asked softly.

My lip trembled and the tears spilled down my cheeks. "She was so precious and so lost. I couldn't just turn away! But now I'm not sure I did the right thing."

Mom gave me a hug and held me as I cried.

Communications with Romania are difficult, at best, and I received little word of how my baby girl was doing. I raised and wired the money for her surgeries, and hoped that it would get to her. I wrote e-mails inquiring about her, but obtained no response. I sent prayers, lots of prayers, to heaven, begging God to watch over my little girl.

Finally, three years later, a letter arrived in the

mail. Recognizing the postmark from Romania, my hands shook as I ripped open the envelope and read the cursive script:

Dear Michelle,

I don't know whether you will remember me; I am one of the mission workers who was here when you were in Iași. I just wanted to tell you that Mihaiela has had her surgery and is currently receiving physiotherapy. Her legs were in casts for a long time, but she is now in a wheelchair to help her around until she can walk properly. She is so proud that she can move around with her friends! She is such a sweet child—whenever new volunteers come or we have people touring the orphanage, we always introduce them to Mihaiela, because she is such an entertainer! She will soon be moving from the orphanage into a private group home that has a family setting. . . .

The letter went on, but my eyes turned to a photo that had fallen out of the envelope. It was a picture of a four-year-old girl clapping her hands in obvious joy. Her eyes were bright and clear, her cheeks rosy, and her smile contagious. How different she was from the baby I had held three years before . . . the baby I had given my heart to.

—*Michelle Peters*

Keep Walking

There's a woman I see on the streets of Portland, Oregon, who moves me in a way that's sometimes embarrassing. After crossing paths with her, I've had to pull the car over to rearrange my emotions; she's made me late for appointments and forced me to end a run before it began. I don't know her name, but I speculate it's Alice or Anita or Lucy. I know she lives nearby, and she is probably in her fifties, maybe even my mom's age. Her hair, auburn and wavy, is neither treated nor cut professionally. Her hands, clenched tight around the metal canes, look like my nana's, with gentle age spots and loose skin that has worked too hard for fifty-something years.

I don't always see her in the same place, but she's always alone and oftentimes drenched in the inexorable Pacific Northwest rain that stops for no one, not even a woman on her way home from the Laundromat with her clean clothes still warm like chocolate chip cookies fresh out of the oven. I know that it's laundry in her bag and not cans of peas or liters of Coke, because I've seen her standing against the dryer, folding each sock and each knit top. The bag swings with each step, like a child in a hammock, as she skims the dirty sidewalks with the sides of her shoes.

Her pace is the same, whether she's on the sidewalk or in a crosswalk, always twice as slow as the city's calculated pace for people to cross the street. The "walk" sign vanishes and is replaced with the blinking "Don't walk" sign before she's even taken four steps, while the cars, growling like animals, exhaust carbon monoxide and their patience. But she keeps walking with one cane down and then another. She keeps walking, even in the face of danger and fear.

More than once, I've come upon her mid-crosswalk. The light has already turned green again and the cars, thank God, have seen her and wait until she makes it to the curb. You can see the driver's eyes shift from the radio or their cell phone to the woman, bent and purposeful, scooting toward her destination.

The first time, my running shoes couldn't tread fast enough to get between her and the cars idling behind the line. I positioned myself, awkwardly, with my arms up like a gate protecting her, the way old men do, if they were raised right, when they walk down the street with their wives. Don't think I'm a saint; you would have done it, too. I know this because I've seen other neighbors with their arms out and the same self-conscious smile, blocking her from harm, sure to wait until she gets both canes and both feet up onto the curb before waving the traffic on. I sat, in my car the last time, and watched and wondered, through my suppressed sobs, if everyone is affected as violently as I am.

She never looks up, only at the rubber capping on the end of each cane. Her feet curl inward in such a way that I'm sure they've been sick for awhile, yet I'm equally sure there was a time when she could run and do cartwheels in the grass. The cane wraps around her wrists like Wonder Woman's bracelets as she scoots deliberately, knowing that after 5,000 lefts or 7,000 rights, she'll be home, to her studio apartment, where she knits and takes her medicine.

This woman ruins me every time fate brings her into my life, even if I look away immediately. I don't know why I see her as often as I do or why she makes it hard for me to breathe, but I trust there is a reason. After I see her, sunrises wake me up in the morning and I can smell the rain that dapples my windshield and curls my ponytail. The paint on an artist's canvas reveals the depth of the painter's stroke, and at the market I'm led to the ingredients of my great-grandmother's homemade bread. I find time to visit a friend in the hospital, feel the warmth of my lover in the darkness, and inhale the delicate fragrance of an infant's skin.

Will I be her friend one day, helping her fold her laundry and making her life easier? Or will she just tenderize me from afar, making only my life easier? Will she continue to just remind me of tiny flowers, and the way my mom and dad smile when I get off a plane? Or of my nana's perfume, or the way my brother's toes look more like my dad's every day? Or will Alice or Anita or Lucy forever be nothing more to me than the epitome of determination, burned like public humiliation or regrets into my mind, reminding me that while we are malleable and soft, nothing is insurmountable?

How can we not be inspired, even in a world so fragile, to keep walking?

—*Gina Daggett*

The Connection

"Mom, your flight is overbooked. Why not take a bump and catch a flight tomorrow," my daughter urged.

Should I stay? It was tempting. In a split second, I made a decision that was to take me on an unforgettable journey.

"No, sweetie. I'm ready to go. Besides, I miss your dad."

The trip to Alaska to visit our daughter's family had been fun, but I was anxious to get home. I hugged my daughter, gripped my cane, and headed down the ramp. It was 11:00 P.M., September 10, 2001.

In the early morning hours, the plane arrived at Seattle's SeaTac airport. An attendant was waiting for me with wheelchair and whisked me off to the gate for my connecting flight. Five hip operations have left me with one leg two inches shorter than the other. Wheelchairs and canes are often a part of my life.

As I waited to board the plane, an announcement came on the public address system:

"All planes are grounded. Everyone report to baggage claim. The airport will be closing."

A shock wave went through me. What was happening? How would I handle my luggage? Where would I go?

Across the aisle, a woman with a cell phone to her ear tells anyone listening that a plane has flown into one of the World Trade Center towers. With growing confusion and fear, I started to gather my things. I felt a tap on my shoulder and turned to look into the worried face of a young Asian woman.

In halting English she said, "Please, could you help me understand?"

My mind was spinning. I thought, *Help you! I don't even know what's going on myself. I'm sixty-five and use a cane. I'm a small-town Midwesterner. How can I help you? I need help myself!* But when I started to speak, the words tumbled out differently.

"I don't know what's happening, but why don't you come with me and we'll figure it out together. My name is Marty."

She smiled. "I am Teresa Lin from Taiwan. Thank you very much."

The immediate tasks for Teresa and me were to

locate our luggage and find a place to stay. That took us the better part of the next eight hours.

During the entire time, there were no televisions turned on and no general announcements in the airport. After two chaotic hours, we finally found our luggage. We got in line at the airline counter to pick up hotel and food vouchers. People with cell phones shared information up and down the line. I tried to explain to Teresa what was happening in New York City and, as I learned from fellow passengers, in Washington, D.C., and Pennsylvania. She didn't seem to understand that flying out of a different airport or even getting a bus, train, or taxi were not options at the moment. I sensed her utter disbelief—and shared it.

Teresa's husband called on her cell phone, urging her to come home. But she refused. Nick and Teresa own a marketing business in Taiwan, with an active European market. The purpose of her trip was to establish American clients, and she was reluctant to give up.

A traveler standing in line noticed that I had difficulty standing and found a wheelchair for me. It was another two hours before it was our turn to pick up accommodation vouchers. As I handed my ticket to the agent, she burst into tears.

"I can't do this right now," she said between sobs and hurried away, leaving us standing there open-mouthed.

We waited forty-five minutes until another agent

came. She was courteous and calm. But because Teresa's flight was not a connecting flight, she apparently didn't qualify for a room voucher. Teresa looked at the agent with disbelief and worry.

Without thinking, I blurted out, "She's traveling with me; she can stay in my room."

By late afternoon, after an incredibly long and tiring day, we settled into our room and watched, transfixed, the horrific scenes on television.

After a couple of hours, Teresa turned from the television with eyes wide and said, "Marty, I think every plane in the United States of America is on the ground!"

That was the beginning of five days and nights with Teresa. I continued to explain the news reports and information from the airline. We talked late into the night and over every meal. Teresa referred to her dictionary, and I gently corrected her pronunciations. We shared our lives, our families, our dreams. We giggled in the coffee shop as I tried to explain the American menu. On those occasions when it was difficult for me to walk, Teresa would get snacks and drinks for us. We would stop at the airline information table in the lobby to get the latest updates.

Back in Iowa, my husband Dave was working around the clock to get me home and Teresa on her way. Every time he got a flight booked, it would be canceled. He decided we needed to get to a smaller airport. Fortunately, Dave has family who live in southern Washington. They gladly came to our rescue and took us to Portland, Oregon. Everyone welcomed Teresa with open arms.

Soon it was time to go our separate ways. Teresa reluctantly decided it was best to go to Los Angeles and then home to Taiwan. I went first to our son's home in San Diego and finally back to Iowa.

Teresa and I had shared a lifetime in those five days. We had come to know and love one another. Since we live on opposite sides of the world, we knew that it was unlikely we would see one another again. As we parted, we both sobbed out promises to write.

And so we have. E-mailed letters and pictures have flown back and forth between Iowa and Taiwan. But the best thing to fly into Iowa is Teresa herself. She is finally taking her business trip and making a special stop in Iowa. We are so excited about seeing each other again. It will be a wonderful reunion, and we are already talking about her and her husband, Nick, visiting next year.

The September 11 terrorist attacks left many of us feeling disconnected and distrustful. But on that day a loving connection was formed between an older American lady and a young Taiwanese businesswoman that will last as long as we live.

—*Marty Dodge*

Passing the Halo

When one of earth's angels drops her halo, it falls in the path of someone worthy of filling her shoes—or rather, her halo. There should be hordes of people running after my mother. She's misplaced her halo again.

Tranquility blankets the room as Mom hobbles in, her cane tapping on the hardwood like Morse code. If, indeed, it were a code, I'd probably discover she is making a slightly off-color joke. Mom sees no reason why anyone forced by the cruel twists of fate to carry a cane can't have a little fun with it. She chuckles to herself as she traps the cat's tail. It takes a special person to laugh in the face of aging.

Just as a cat befriends the only person in the room who hates cats, diseases seem to select their unlikely victims. My mom has always led an active life. She didn't watch soap operas, lunch at the country club, or play golf and tennis. She ran seven miles every weekday morning with our arthritic Labrador and skied fourteen miles cross-country most Saturday mornings in the winter. Every Sunday she baked twelve loaves of bread, because her husband liked the smell. When my youngest brother and I were safely launched into high school, she went back to work as a nurse. She was a busy, nonconformist mom.

I've been reaching for her halo all my life. The closest I've come is getting out of bed before my family and making sure the kitchen is clean when they come downstairs.

Mom attended university at night "for something to do." I have issues with that. I have one teenager. At the time, she had four. I have trouble getting the laundry done, let alone writing a thesis. She studied hermeneutics, the science of the interpretation of biblical text. On my eternal quest for her halo, I shall never study hermeneutics, which I find difficult to even spell without using spell check.

Alzheimer's is a random, unpredictable, insidious disease. Without discretion, it is diminishing one of the most intelligent women I know—my mom.

The phrase "the long good-bye" was popularized during former President Reagan's public battle with Alzheimer's disease. In my mom's case, it's been more like a quick adieu. When Dad couldn't find the stove knob, she smiled and said, "Why didn't you ask me sooner?" as she shuffled to the linen closet to retrieve it.

"The runner" is how our family doctor remembers Mom. After years of treating her body like a temple, her hips have degenerated and left her crippled. Her sense of humor allows her to rise above the encumbrances of her golden years. Now, she can have a cane for poking at cats and passersby as she sits in her chair, exhausted from her trip to the bathroom. Maybe that's where she left her halo.

Mom's hip surgery was scheduled for a cold Tuesday morning in November. The hospital admitting staff was swift and courteous, even more so, it seemed, on discovering that Mom was a retired nurse.

The surgery itself was uneventful. My dad and I met her on the third floor, where, to our delight, she was installed in a private room directly across from the busy nursing station. As the afternoon wore on, Mom seemed a little dazed, but there was nothing really out of the ordinary. Spencer, my strong, quiet, ever-wise older brother, joined Dad and me in our vigil. We all took turns sitting beside Mom, stroking her arm and talking to her. Every so often she wakened, smiled her knowing, gentle smile, and drifted back to sleep.

I arrived at the hospital the next morning to a flurry of activity outside Mom's door. I watched the frantic bustle of nurses rushing in and out of her room. With trepidation, I approached the nurses'

station. Mom's blood pressure had dropped danger-
ously low and her hemoglobin count was half what it
should have been. Dad and I, being inexperienced in
all things medical, stood in the hall and anxiously
watched the proceedings. The efficient staff scurried
around, setting up blood and saline solutions for
transfusion. I had no idea what the saline was for,
and so I asked. The nurse, Lynn, patiently explained
it to me, two or three times, because in my frightened
state the English language and all cognitive functions seemed to have abandoned me.

We spent the day watching the thick red blood
drop steadily into Mom's small arm, while the
machines beeped incessantly. She slept through most
of it. Finally, by early afternoon, things seemed to have
calmed down, and she was declared stable again.

After a harrowing, sleepless night, I made the two-
hour trip back to the small town that had become
Mom's temporary home. Dad had arrived before me.
He looked pale and tired. Obviously, he hadn't slept
much more than I had. Mom looked decidedly better.

When I entered Mom's palatial private room the
next morning, I was relieved to see her being helped
onto her bed by Lynn, the nurse who had so thoughtfully explained the saline to me. Mom was fully
dressed and looked ready to take on the world.

"Come on, sweetie, move your arse back," Lynn's
big cheery voice boomed out of her diminutive body.

Turning to me, Lynn said, "She's so cute." Her happy smile matched her words.

My strict British upbringing made me cringe at the word "arse." Though the word startled me, it was spoken with kindness and compassion. Still, I didn't know how Mom would react. We hadn't even been allowed to mention passing wind while we were growing up! I glanced over Lynn's small, strong shoulder to gauge Mom's reaction. She didn't even notice. I shrugged it off and smiled back at Lynn.

Throughout the day, Lynn hustled up and down the halls, wearing out the soles of her battered tennis shoes. Every time she rushed into Mom's room, she would pause as though taking a well-needed rest, smile, and slow her manner. As she tended to her patient and straightened the covers, she'd chat and stroke Mom's arm. Best of all, in her too-big-for-her-body voice, Lynn passed cheer and goodwill straight from her heart to Mom's.

Lynn was protective of Mom. When she was in charge, she was truly in charge. Mom seemed to be a favorite, and it was magical for me, as her child, to watch the bond forming between these two nurses.

Mom's confusion deepened after the surgery. Initially it was blamed on the anesthetic. I, being a medical neophyte, had no idea how that could be, since she'd had an epidural, which is a local rather than a general anesthetic. Later, as the confusion continued,

it was blamed on the morphine, and so it was with-
drawn—not that it did any good; Mom couldn't
remember to depress the button on her IV to admin-
ister the much-needed pain relief. She was switched
to Tylenol-3. The confusion lingered.

Sunday morning I arrived to find Mom in a state
of agitation.

"When is your Dad getting here?" she asked me
in hushed tones, glancing around to see if anyone
could overhear our conversation.

"I don't know. I told him to stay at the hotel and
catch up on his rest. He's not feeling very well.
Why?" I replied as casually as possible.

"He's going to be mad at me, isn't he?" she asked.

"Why?" I asked.

"He knows I robbed the bank, doesn't he? Did he
tell anyone else? I hope he doesn't tell them. He is
going to be mad."

My stomach lurched. My eyes stung with unshed
tears. My biggest fear was becoming a reality. Her
Alzheimer's was rearing its ugly head.

"Mom, good people don't rob banks. You're a
good person. You didn't do anything wrong," I said,
as calmly as I could.

"I did. The teller told me they were going to
change my medication." She whispered in a conspir-
atorial voice.

When she'd drifted off to sleep, I crept out of the

room to find out what was going on. Lynn was off duty, so I spoke with the nurse who was caring for my mother. She said they had reduced her medication again in an effort to clear her thinking, but she was puzzled about Mom's reaction.

I asked if Mom had misbehaved during the night. No. Had she done something and been scolded for it? No. Had someone spoken sharply to her? No.

Dad arrived. After twenty minutes in Dad's presence, it was as though a fog had lifted. Mom was lucid again.

The next day, Mom wanted to phone her brother Gill. Uncle Gill died thirty years ago.

On Monday, Mom was scheduled for transfer to her small hometown hospital. She was up, dressed, and ready to go by eight o'clock in the morning. Dad went ahead to get everything "set up" for her at the other end. It is a two-and-a-half-hour drive, so we encouraged Dad to leave early. Two hours after Dad had left, the receiving hospital called to say it had no beds available. We would have to try again tomorrow.

The waiting game had started. Spencer drove up for a visit the next day. I drove up on Friday, determined to camp out for as long as it took to get Mom safely loaded into the ambulance. Finally, the call came; there was a bed. Lynn rushed off to book an ambulance before anyone could change his or her mind.

The ambulance attendants arranged Mom onto the gurney. Lynn came to inspect. Like a mother bird, she rechecked all the straps. Discreetly, she pointed out to the attendants that Mom had Alzheimer's, imparting this information in a manner that protected the dignity of her charge.

As they began to roll Mom away, Lynn put out her hand to stop them.

"Hang on," she commanded. She bent over Mom's stretcher again. "Okay, sweetie, you're off to the new hospital. I want you to be good, okay? I'm going to come up to see you on my motorcycle soon, okay? Don't give them a hard time on the ride. I told them to hit some potholes, just to keep you on your toes." She smiled fondly down at Mom.

Relief filled Mom's face upon hearing the familiar, larger-than-life voice. Mom had been afraid and confused again, and the only one who had noticed was Lynn. Comforted, Mom was now ready to go.

Tears of gratitude shone in my eyes. But I didn't stop to thank the little nurse with the biggest heart. So I will now.

Thank you, Lynn.

Now I know what happened to Mom's halo. Lynn picked it up.

—*Anna Therien*

Corinna's Quilts

Soft, golden curls dangled from his muscle-padded arms as he carried her lifeless body through the emergency entrance. He was a former football star, a wrestling champ, and his children's hero, but now he was helpless. All he could do was wait.

Bryan Jones paced around the waiting room like a fenced thoroughbred while Mary Jones prayed in the corner. Why were they here? What had gone wrong? How could their healthy, happy, always-doing-gymnastics, four-year-old daughter collapse without warning?

Doctors opened the young body to do an emergency appendectomy only to discover a twisted, kinked small intestine, packed with gangrene infection. Nothing could be done to save her. They closed the incision.

"There is nothing we can do," they said. "She won't last long."

The horrified parents would not give up, nor would they consider letting her give up. Clinging to faith, they prayed. All night they prayed. All of her siblings prayed along with every relative and friend they knew.

Corinna's doctor could not sleep that night. The image of her sweet face, smiling up at him from a nest of blond curls resting on a white hospital pillow made a vivid projection in his mind every time he closed his eyes. The next morning he requested another look. To his amazement, the remaining sixty centimeters of bad bowel had revived. If only it would be enough.

The days and months that followed were painful, yet miraculous. Corinna and her parents never lost faith. She was in and out of numerous hospitals over the next several years. Always, she entered with a smile, her favorite doll, and a heavy dose of hope. Life-flight experts rushed her to the Primary Children's Medical Center in Utah. Later, she was sent by jet plane to a specialized hospital in Omaha, Nebraska, for an experimental small bowel transplant. She missed birthday parties and was hospitalized in the far-away states during several holidays.

In December 1995, neighborhood friends in Rexburg, Idaho, surprised Corinna's family and her special friend, Cassie, with an early Christmas gift of airplane tickets for each of them to visit Corinna. Every moment of the three-day trip was planned to perfection.

Halloween was celebrated on the first day. Because Corinna could not be moved, all of her siblings—Lydia, Clarissa, Victoria, Talon, and Kjel—stood around her bed, wearing colorful costumes. Corinna hid behind a disguise of mustache and silly eyeglasses. Every time a knock came at the door, they shouted "trick or treat," and a nurse or doctor would enter with candy for their bags.

The second day was Thanksgiving. Cassie, a college-age friend who filled in at home while Corinna's daddy was at work and her mommy was at the hospital, helped cook a Thanksgiving turkey at the Ronald McDonald House. Corinna was too ill to eat, but she loved having her family near. "I have so much to be thankful for," she said.

On the last day, Corinna's daddy hauled in Christmas gifts as if he were Santa Claus. The joy and love the family shared in the hospital room blessed them with cherished memories and gifts that money could never buy.

Corinna learned about feeding tubes, oxygen apparatuses, and hepron locks. She endured repeated surgeries, including several transplants. Always, Corinna's mommy was by her side. She was there while she was expecting little Ben, and then later when she was nursing him. Such scenes were repeated when baby Joseph came along, as well.

Two weeks after her first transplant, Corinna

vomited during a routine medical procedure, and the vomit aspirated into her lungs. Serious damage resulted. Chest tubes were used, twelve at a time, to drain the fluids. A feeding tube led directly to her stomach, and a ventilator helped her breathe during the eight weeks she struggled for her life in the pediatric intensive care unit.

A package from Grandma Billings was waiting when Corinna awoke. It was a snuggly homemade quilt for Corinna's hospital room. She studied its happy lamb pictures and colorful pattern. It was comforting to her. She wrapped it around her, pretending she was in her grandma's arms. Corinna loved it. The quilt, like her doll, became her constant companion.

Somehow, Corinna managed to keep up with her schoolwork. She was gifted with artistic and creative abilities, too. During long recovery stays in the Ronald McDonald House, she and Mom found fun things to do for others. She made gifts and cards for other patients and for family and friends at home.

Then, one day, Corinna had a beautiful idea: *Every child in the hospital should have a snuggly, cuddly quilt to love.*

That's when Miss Corinna Jones went to work. Her wish was to donate new, colorful, snuggly cuddle quilts to the pediatric unit in the University of Nebraska Medical Center. Each hospitalized child could choose a homey quilt for his or her bed. After each child's stay in the hospital, the quilt would be sanitized and used to cheer another visitor.

Corinna wrote letters and made phone calls, inviting everyone she could think of to help with her quilt project. She and her mom set up a portable sewing machine in an empty room of the Ronald McDonald basement. There, they not only made more quilts, but they also gave sewing lessons to other mothers and patients, from various countries around the world.

Quilts began to arrive. Corinna's project was contagious. Everyone wanted to help. Aunts, cousins, neighbors, friends, church groups, and youth organizations donated stacks of cheerful quilts. Her Grandma Billings sent fifty quilts. A young women's group in Omaha tied more than a hundred quilts for Corinna; one of the girls tied twenty-five quilts by herself. While looking for quilting fabric at garage sales, another mother explained the project to a homeowner, who donated an armload of material from her basement.

When Corinna left the hospital, its closets were bursting with quilts. Today, a framed photo of Corinna hangs by the nurses' station above a caption explaining her quilt project:

"When you are having a hard day, wrap yourself up in one of these quilts and that will be a hug for you from Corinna."

Today, Corinna Jones is a healthy teenager who lives a normal life and continues to keep the children's hospital supplied with quilted hugs—proving that laughter, love, and service to others are truly the best medicine.

—Susan B. Mitchell

The Journey of
Jake and Dora

My great-grandparents, Jake and Dora, were born in two different villages in Lithuania. At that time, Lithuania belonged to Russia, and the Lithuanians, especially the Jews, faced persecution under the Russian tsar. Jake and Dora dreamed of freedom and the opportunity for a better life.

They married when he was eighteen and she seventeen. They had little money and planned to leave for America right after the wedding. Eager to begin their new life right away, Jake applied for the passports. His request was denied because he had not served in the Russian Army. Unwilling to give up, Jake found an agent who, for a price, could provide him with the necessary passports. They managed to scrape together the money and were on their way.

They traveled as steerage passengers. After a grueling trip, they arrived in Canada and traveled by train to the lower east side of New York City. Their destination was the apartment of Dora's brother, Harry, and they held tight to the scrap of paper with his last known address.

It was late at night when they finally arrived. Jake knocked on the door. There was no answer. He knocked again, but no one was home. There was little money left, and Jake and Dora decided it would be best if they could get some sleep before figuring out what to do next. Exhausted from their journey, they lay down in the hallway outside Harry's door and quickly fell asleep.

Before daylight, they were awakened by a tenant who stumbled over them as he groped his way to the toilet. The man yelled out, calling them drunkards and bums. The noise awakened the other tenants on the floor, who rushed out of their flats to see what was going on at that unearthly hour. Jake explained who they were and why they had decided to sleep in the hallway. The tenants were *landsleit*, people who came from the same or nearby towns in their home country. They welcomed Jake and Dora, fed them, and informed them that Harry had moved to Harlem. One of the neighbors gave them the new address.

Jake and Dora rented a two-room flat on the Lower East Side. The flat, like those of their neighbors, was barely fit for human habitation. The rooms were small, overcrowded, dark, and poorly ventilated. The building was infested with cockroaches, bedbugs, flies, mosquitoes, mice, and rats. Dora would heat water in pans until the water boiled, and then she would throw the boiling liquid to try and drown the cockroaches that crawled on the kitchen walls. Jake used the flame from a gas pipe to burn the bedbugs.

Jake and Dora's building did not have the luxury of a toilet in the hallway; they had a tiny, windowless outhouse in the yard. It was dark and often dirty and smelly. There were no washbasins or paper towels. Newspapers, old telephone books, and fruit wrappers were used as toilet paper.

Jake needed to find work; however, he knew no trade other than farming. In Lithuania, his family had farmed a large estate owned by the nobility. The knowledge of farming was of no value in the ghetto. After discussing the possibilities at length with his neighbors, Jake was convinced that he should become a custom tailor in the women's coat and suit industry. He saw the validity of their simple argument: "Women will always need coats and suits." He became an apprentice in a shop, earning two dollars a week. In time, Jake's skills improved, as did his salary. He found employment with better clothing establishments: Lord and Taylor, Franklin Simon, and Levine and Smith.

Jake and Dora were eager to begin their family in

America. Their first child was a girl who died soon after birth from rickets. Next, they had a son. He died from croup when he was just six years old. With so little money to buy nourishing food and in such meager living conditions, a child would need to be strong to survive. Jake and Dora desperately wanted children, and finally, Abraham was born, followed by Ida, and then Meyer.

To earn extra money, Jake rented a pushcart on Ludlow Street for twenty-five cents a day and loaded it with apples, pears, oranges, or grapes, which he bought from wholesalers across the street. He pushed the cart through the streets to Little Italy and sold the fruit to Italian immigrants. Summers in the city were uncomfortably hot, and the winter wind was downright painful. There was no bathroom to use, and his legs would grow tired. On a good day, he could earn a profit of about two dollars.

When the children grew a bit older, Dora took a job as a cook with a catering establishment. Her income helped augment Jake's meager wages and paid for some of the luxuries they craved—a dress and shoes for Ida, jackets or pants for Abe and Meyer, a radio for the house.

Jake was literate: He read and wrote Yiddish; he read Hebrew; he spoke Polish, Russian, Lithuanian, Latvian, and some German. Dora could neither read nor write any language, but she spoke all languages that her husband did. They knew that education would help their children to achieve a better lifestyle. The importance of learning was never far from the hearts and minds of the people of the ghetto.

Jake and Dora remained focused on their wish to build new and better lives for themselves and their children. They had two goals: to work hard and to get good educations for their children. The children were never permitted to forget these goals and always held fast to the belief that economic and social success was a possibility. Through hard work and education, they could earn their passports out of the ghetto.

The children read library books, secondhand books, cheap editions of the great books bought at Woolworth's, and the Bible. In the public schools, they studied hard and posed few disciplinary problems. On the streets of the ghetto, children learned about prejudice, sex, and crime. They learned to haggle for what they bought, and they learned to survive. Many, like my grandma Ida, developed a deep desire to get out of the ghetto.

Ida did leave. She earned a Ph.D. and became an extraordinary educator as well as a devoted wife and mother. Her daughters followed her lead and built successful careers and marriages of their own. Although they would never know of the struggles and hardships their grandparents had endured, Ida's daughters had been bequeathed their values of hard work and the importance of education. And so have their children—Jake and Dora's great-grandchildren—who have attended prestigious universities such as Harvard, Princeton, the Massachusetts Institute of Technology, the California Institute of Technology, and the College of William and Mary.

For Ida's ninetieth birthday party, the family gathered to celebrate. There was plenty of food and colorful decorations. For entertainment, one of the grandchildren made a slideshow; another took pictures and promised to e-mail everyone a copy. Before the festivities ended, a cell phone rang. It was Jackie, Ida's daughter, who lived in California and had been unable to make it to the party. As Ida chatted with Jackie on the cell phone, it was difficult to believe that she'd grown up in the ghetto, the daughter of poor, uneducated Lithuanian immigrants. Then again, maybe it is not so difficult—as long as you believe, as Jack and Dora did, that dreams really do come true.

—*Valerie L. Merahn*

With a Little Boost from My Friends

"Now don't tell her we're coming. We want it to be a surprise," my friend Linda said.

"Okay, I won't tell her," my husband, Tim, whispered into the phone, but then had second thoughts. "No, I'll have to say something, so she can get dressed. She'd be embarrassed if she were in her bathrobe."

"That's true," Linda said. "Hey, we want to bring lunch, too. What's she eating these days?"

"Hmmm. Not much. Tuna, white rice, asparagus. That's about it lately."

"Perfect. We'll set up a little picnic on your patio."

"She'll like that. But don't make her laugh too much. It hurts when she laughs."

"Yeah, I know. See you tomorrow."

Linda hung up and called Denise, Stacy, and Jan to let them know everything was on. It's difficult to be a friend to someone who's been sick, especially when she's been sick for months and is a classic "type A personality" who is fiercely independent and unused to being down. But my friends are faithful, accepting, and patient—the perfect combination.

My birthday dawned like any other day for me. I'd been in bed for six months with a malady that had left me with chronic stomach pain. Unable to eat a regular diet, my weight had dropped from 130 to under 100 pounds. Sitting for any period of time became impossible. My days were spent in bed listening to the sounds from the grammar school that my children attended across the street.

At times I was grateful for my isolation. I was proud, and I didn't want people to see me in my starved state. Their looks of concern and empathy were genuine, but I didn't want to be a source of sadness for anyone. My friend Linda was different. She knew instinctively that I didn't want to be pitied. A few days before my birthday, she'd taken me to a local shop to get me out of the house for awhile. Linda thought it would be fun to try on sunglasses. To show her I didn't need any, I pulled a pair out of my purse that I had bought previous to getting sick.

"Put them on," she said. I did. Linda's face turned red, and she laughed the kind of laugh that makes those around her laugh, too.

"What?" I defended. "I like these sunglasses."

"Binsey, they're huge!" she said.

"No, they're not," I said, looking for my reflection in the mirror. She was right. They were huge. We laughed again.

"Well," Linda offered, "you know you've lost too much weight when your sunglasses are too big." We laughed some more. Linda loved me—no matter what.

Linda, Denise, Stacy, and Jan arrived around noon for my birthday "surprise." They trounced in— Denise giggling, Linda hugging, Stacy grinning, Jan laughing—their arms loaded with gifts and bowls of food. They knew I knew they were coming, but we all acted like I didn't.

We sat on the patio and enjoyed a gourmet meal of tuna, asparagus, and white rice. I opened some thoughtful gifts, and then I was pulled to my feet and led into my living room for the best present I've ever received. Giggling nervously, Denise put a video into the VCR.

On the screen appeared all of my friends' children, singing "Happy Birthday, Binsey" from several locations. Next, my friends' husbands did the same. Then came greetings from many other friends and acquaintances who had gathered for another event. A birthday cake had been made for me, and the candles were lit and blown out from off-camera at the appropriate moment. Next, I was treated to a song from the Book of Psalms, sung and accompanied on the guitar by two people I loved dearly. Tears filled my eyes and spilled over. I was so surprised and touched by all the love expressed. But what came next was so unexpected, so out of the ordinary, to say I was blown away would be an understatement.

Every year our town hosts an event for serious bicyclists. The thirty-mile ride goes right through the center of town and attracts hundreds of riders in bright, colorful riding suits. Traffic is directed by uniformed policemen with whistles and waving arms. Whatever possessed Denise to stand on that busy corner with video camera in hand is still a mystery to me. But I'm so grateful she did. For next to appear on the video were several riders, who, in the middle of their race, stopped to wish me a happy birthday and good health.

Even the stocky police officer took the time during a lull in riders to add some humor. "You say your friend has been in bed for six months? What I want to know is: Who has she been in bed with?"

I laughed, a lot. It hurt, but it was worth it.

But Denise wasn't finished. The grand finalé was the firemen. Tall and strong, all lined up in front of the fire engine at our local firehouse, they sang "Happy Birthday" with such gusto, I laughed and cried at the same time. I was so stunned and deeply touched by my friends' extravagant gift of love that I was speechless for several minutes, before I finally choked out my appreciation.

I remained ill for many months after the Binsey birthday extravaganza, but a new doctor and an accurate diagnosis eventually put me on the road to recovery. I even went back to work.

My coworkers are special people, and we've become very supportive of each other. A few weeks ago our dynamic general manager had a freak accident at home that left him with serious head trauma. The night of the accident, surgery was performed to relieve brain swelling. The ensuing four weeks in the intensive care unit meant no visitors or even flowers.

Once he was moved out of ICU, his wife warned us that his memory gaps could make visits embarrassing. We were at a loss at what to do. Then I remembered there had been a time when I, too, was embarrassed to have visitors, when I, too, wanted to hide from the good intentions of others. And I knew that it was time to make another video. A video filled with greetings and best wishes from friends and coworkers and, of course, a few thoughtful strangers as well.

—*Binsey Coté*

Errands of Honor

Mamie stepped from the steamy summer heat of 1954 into the refreshing air-conditioned lobby of City Bank. Immediately, the bank president greeted her and offered his sympathy at the passing of a respected man, a man whose word was as good as his bond. When she had been seated in a private room, Mamie opened the safe deposit box. Mamie reached for the watch, her father's words echoing in her mind: "Give the watch to his oldest child."

Caressing its satin gold finish, she turned the watch over and over in her palm as her memory traveled back to the year of her father's broken leg. . . .

David Gettys stopped abruptly in the middle of the dusty road as the rabbit dashed across. It reached a safe distance, looked back, and skittered into the field of purple-top turnips. *That rabbit heard me coming up the road*, he thought.

He drank in the dew-damp morning, sniffed the honeysuckle air. He watched the world awaken along the brightening edge of its black-bowl sky. He had started out at first light, to catch the coolest part of that September day. His errand was important, to pay a debt.

That year, 1931, was a good one on his South Carolina farm. Crops were almost ready for harvest. The garden had been profitable. Late the day before, Mr. McPherson made the largest vegetable purchase yet. A shortage of change had left twenty-five cents due.

"Don't have the right change, Mr. McPherson, but I will tomorrow."

His word was as good as his bond. The walk to McPherson's house was long but not sufficient to harness his mule, Jere. Besides, it was Sunday, the day of rest, and even his mule deserved Sunday off.

Trudging along pot-holed Route 2, his sturdy physique and easy stride belied his sixty-six years, mostly spent ranching, wrestling, and farming. Even so, his loss of the world of sound seemed like cruel robbery. But there were always the sounds in his head, the ballads he sang when the silence got too lonely.

He picked up his rabbit-interrupted pace and thought of his property, land he had fiercely held. Now, the Great Depression had spread across the country. He could feed his family while others stood in food lines. Life was good.

Ah, Mamie, he mused. His nine-year-old daughter and only child was the best thing that had happened between him and his wife, Mary. Not bad for an old man.

He passed the plum tree and noticed a trembling limb. A nervous wren had lit deftly on its lower branch. His memory heard it chattering, and he smiled.

The sun crept up the edge of the East pasture at a pace visually measurable, and suddenly it freed the horizon in a leap, like a ball bouncing into place. It held his gaze.

The sun comes up like thunder, he thought. *Like thunder!*

Suddenly, the ground rumbled behind him. He turned to look and his eyes widened in terror. *Motorcar!* Too close to dodge. The big metal machine charged like a bull. He tried to jump from its path, and the driver tried to swerve. Both misjudged. The machine won.

David Gettys lay motionless, his mouth full of dirt, wondering whether he was still alive. His leg left no doubt, as it screamed out to him in knifelike pain. He spit, then grit his teeth over the remaining gravel. He struggled to raise his body from the road, but fell back just as a huge man knelt at his side.

Big Early, a sharecropper, as strong as a wrestler,

too, had seen the accident from his porch. He lifted David Gettys and placed him into the car that had struck him, and the driver quickly drove back to the Gettys' farm. David would remember little about the car or the driver.

Early lifted him out of the car, cradling him as gently as a baby, and carefully climbed the porch steps.

Mrs. Gettys swung wide the front door as Early carried her husband into the house and placed him on their bed.

"Mary, my leg's broke."

Mamie stood by, wide-eyed with alarm. She had never seen her father in pain and certainly never helpless. David ached with humiliation, to be carried.

Dr. Walker was quick to respond to a neighbor's summons. He made the house call in his own car and transported his patient himself to the Phillips Infirmary. Mary and Mamie rode along. The patient refused to lose consciousness.

A pragmatic Irish roar echoed through the hospital corridors. "Go easy on my pocketbook, boys!"

The leg was set. The farmer went home.

When he complained of his foot getting cold, Mary filled a quart jar with water boiled on the wood stove, fitted the rubber ring at its mouth, and screwed the metal disc and ring on tightly. She wrapped it with rags and placed it next to his foot.

Frustration soon drove the farmer to his feet and determination kept him there. He swung himself between the self-hewn boards of the crutches, which his wife had padded, his cast-encased leg dangling and his spirit wilting.

Crops ripened.

The cast felt like an anchor, and the weeks that followed were heavy with worry. Would he lose his crops? Fear is far more wearisome than work. Harvest time was usually hard but joyous work, that wonderful season of reaping.

The entire Gettys household could have been stone deaf, what for the silence at their breakfast table. The morning air, usually fresh and invigorating, seemed to hang stale, threatening defeat.

After a morose interval, David broke the silence.

"The best crops we've had in years might be lost. Lost! And why? Because of a tornado? A flood? A hail storm? An infestation?"

Like an iron mallet, his fist came down on the table.

"No! All because of a confounded broken leg! If those crops aren't brought in soon, it'll be too late."

His tone was dejected. But personal disasters such as his are not overlooked among other farmers.

That day his nephew Gillam arrived from the next county with a wagon and team of mules. They spent the afternoon getting in the corn. Mary and Mamie walked, one to each side of Gillam's wagon. The process was smooth: Break off an ear and, with a sweeping motion of the same arm, toss it into the wagon. Break, toss. Break, toss. Break, toss. They stayed with the chore row after row until all five acres of corn were harvested.

Within the week, neighbors started turning out to help. Soon, every Gettys field was harvested. Only one person was noticeably absent—the driver of the motorcar.

Days of autumn turned toward Thanksgiving, and the air comfortably cool. Perfect for porch sitting. The cast was off, but the leg weak. David Gettys tried to hide the limp as he joined Mamie on the front porch, settling onto the bottom step and resting his feet on the neatly swept yard.

Mamie picked up the mink-black cat and snuggled it beneath her right arm as she backed up to the swing behind the trumpet vine trellis. She loosely dangled one leg as the other pumped against the floor of the porch. Mary, observing her own rule, quietly closed the screen door. She took her place on the step, next to David, adjusting her dress as she sat, letting it fall far over her knees. She picked at it, pinch-like, then smoothed the apron over it. Satisfied, she rested her hands, palms up, in her lap.

"We've enough laid by for ourselves and the

stock and then some," the farmer projected loudly enough to hear himself. He stretched his back almost straight, then relaxed and let each hand rest over its knee. On his land he felt a sense of peace.

A sailor-pink sky framed the garden. Next to it something edged into sight, something black, coming up the drive. He couldn't hear it but he instantly recognized its ugly face.

"Now, what in devil's name is going on?"

This time, the mechanical monster moved very slowly and stopped. A man got out of the driver's side. His black suit so closely matched his skin that, against the sunset, he formed a silhouette. He was dressed in his best, his shirt freshly laundered, wearing probably his only necktie. A woman remained in the passenger seat. Children in the back seat, wide-eyed, pressed their faces against the window. All were dressed in their ceremonial best.

The man walked slowly and deliberately, as if trying to make footprints in that hard Carolina clay. His arms hung at his side, his fists clenched like knots. He approached cautiously and then stood only inches from the weakened leg.

The swing stopped. The black cat leapt away.

"Mr. Gettys, I been studyin over the accident, bout yo doctor bills and hospital bills. An I heard bout yo trouble gettin the crops in, what with you laid up with yo laig. I ain't got nothin but my car and

I owes the bank for it."

He knew to shout, but even if his words weren't heard, his face spoke of his guilt and dilemma.

He extended his arm, fisted palm down. His body leaned anxiously forward, as if the arm needed a push. The palm turned upward. Ebony fingers opened to uncover a gleaming gold-plated pocket watch.

The farmer hesitated, looking at the prized item that every man dreamed of owning. He lifted his gaze from the gold into the tormented eyes of its owner.

Slowly, he reached and took the watch.

The man, as if relieved of a heavy burden, turned and left, walking taller.

That night at dinner, David said, "Mary, that watch goes into our safe deposit box. I don't need two gold watches."

"Why don't you just sell it?"

"No, it's priceless. When I die, I want Mamie to take the watch to that man's oldest child, along with the telling of this story. I want her to say that it's a story about a man who did the right thing."

—*Mary Stripling*

The Gloved Guitarist of Tossa de Mar

Tossa de Mar is a small tourist town in Spain. During the summer months, it is busy with tourists, but being in the northeast part of the country, where it is cool from October through April, most of the residents of Tossa who own or work in the town's hotels, bars, and restaurants must find work elsewhere.

A middle-aged man called Ramon Delgado owns one of the bars. In his younger days, Ramon was one of the best-known flamenco guitarists in the whole of Spain. He traveled all over Europe and even to South America. He made records and appeared on many television shows. When he decided to settle down, he bought a bar in his hometown of Tossa, which he and his family run.

Every evening during the tourist season, as the sun slowly sets, Ramon gets out his guitar and entertains the customers sitting at little wooden tables inside and outside his bar, often asking for requests. Year after year, people have come to his bar to hear him play his guitar and sing.

Even in his fifties, Ramon was a handsome man and still took great care of his skillful hands. He kept them supple with special herbal creams, and he never undertook anything that might risk damaging his hands.

During the relatively short tourist season of May to early October, Ramon and his compadres would open early in the morning and close late in the evening, to try to make as much money as they could while the tourists were there.

In the years 1994 to 1997, the summer weather in Tossa de Mar was poor, with many windy and rainy days, which is very unusual for that part of Spain. Consequently, many of the tourists who had experienced a poor summer one year did not return the next. A number of these tourists, largely from the United Kingdom, went to Florida in the United States, instead. It didn't cost that much more, and the warm weather was more or less guaranteed.

The loss of business made it even more imperative for the residents of Tossa de Mar to find alternative work during the winter. Some drove the hour and a half to Barcelona every morning and again home every evening. Barcelona is a big and busy city, though, and many of the people from Tossa disliked working there.

One afternoon the winter of 1996, a terrible storm struck La Costa Brava, the brunt of it slamming into tiny Tossa de Mar. The skies grew black; the winds blew stronger than any ever recorded in the Catalonia region of Spain. Huge waves slammed into the buildings on the seafront, damaging many of the apartments and a few of the restaurants.

One of the restaurants was nearly demolished. It belonged to a man in his early seventies named Carlos Calero. Carlos lost two sons to the sea in 1975, when their fishing boat sank in a storm off Costa Brava. His two daughters helped him run the restaurant.

Once the storm had passed, the townspeople went down to the seafront to see how bad the damage was. They all stared in horror at Carlos Calero and his wrecked restaurant. The front wall had collapsed into rubble, and the interior was badly water damaged. Distraught, the poor old man stood helplessly, shaking his head and biting back tears.

Tossa is small and its residents are close. Although they all compete for tourist business during the summer season, there is no rivalry between them. They all gathered around Carlos and assured him that all was not lost. They would help him.

First, they immediately made his restaurant

windproof and watertight. Then, as soon as the weather improved, they got to work. All those who were painting or fixing their own establishments and all those who were working on buildings to make extra money put aside some time and worked extra hours to help old Carlos repair his restaurant. So many people gave a couple of hours here and a few hours there that not one day went by without someone working on Carlos's restaurant.

One sunny day in early March, I walked past Carlos's restaurant. Plasterwork was being done inside, while Manuel Desabio and his brother laughed as they repaired the brick exterior walls. Enrique, from a large bar around the corner, was in paint-splattered overalls, painting the kitchen doors. Most touching of all, though, was Ramon Delgado, the flamenco guitarist, who, though unskilled in any building trade, was nonetheless moving bricks and doing what he could to assist the others. Of course, he wore a pair of gloves to protect his famous hands. He got teased about being a señora, but he was there, helping out.

By the start of tourist season in early May, Carlos Calero's restaurant was up and running again. The wonderful thing is, none of the many who had helped save it from ruin thought they had done anything out of the ordinary. A member of their community needed help, and they gave it freely—without a second thought, without being asked, and without patting themselves on the back. Their reward was in sharing a sense of achievement in having managed to save the place.

On opening night, Carlos invited everyone who had helped repair the restaurant over for some food and a glass of wine or two. His daughters cooked up all the favorite local dishes, and Carlos gave a little speech. He thanked his friends for saving his restaurant, and he thanked God for giving him such wonderful friends. Once the meal was under way, Ramon Delgado, minus his gloves, picked up his guitar and sent his lovely music floating into the warm night air.

—Joyce Stark

Snow Angel

Lillian and Mom came late to their friendship.

Both widowed, they met and their relationship bloomed when Lillian moved to Lafayette, about a block away from Mom's house. When arthritis ended Mom's daily walks to the post office, Lillian, who loved to walk, volunteered to pick up her mail and bring it right to the house.

Thus began their daily chats over coffee.

Very few days passed during the next ten years that Lillian didn't walk up the back alley and across Mom's yard to her back door. Watching through the kitchen window, Mom set the mugs out the moment she spotted her friend. Lillian laid the mail on the table, pulled Mom into a hug, then sat at the kitchen table to tell the news she had heard at the post office. Mom filled in the background stories.

Lillian spoke in awe of how Mom knew everyone in the township. A fifth-generation native, Mom knew just about everyone, their family histories and secrets.

Lillian had always been an "outsider." Having moved to the area during World War II, as a working mother, battered wife, and then a divorcee, she was out of step with the conservative farming community.

The two friends would sip and talk a while. Looking at the clock, they would start making plans for lunch. Usually they called a couple of other widows in town. Everyone would pile into Mom's car to head for a favorite restaurant. Eventually Lillian took over the driving, since she was younger, seventy-something to Mom's eighty-something.

They plotted back-road routes that were free of traffic and didn't require the left turns Lillian dreaded. It never failed that Mom met someone at the restaurant she hadn't seen for a long time, and Lillian would add a new acquaintance to her growing list.

Over the years, Lillian, a flighty, small-boned, birdlike woman, shrunk even smaller. Mom baked and cooked and offered her special treats.

"I made some of those cookies you like," Mom would say as she accepted her morning mail. "They'll taste good with the coffee."

Lillian would usually take a bite and say, "Oh, Gladys, you'll have to give me the recipe."

They both knew she wouldn't bake any cookies, and they knew that Lillian would take only one bite, never two.

One cold November day, Mom worried and paced. Lillian had been rushed to the hospital. They talked on the phone, and friends took her to visit, but she knew that Lillian's "thin" had turned to frail.

Several friends and family members began bringing Mom's mail. But two weeks later when Lillian came home from the hospital, she phoned to say, "I'll be there tomorrow with your mail. Just so you know and don't let anyone else get it."

Mom protested. "It's cold out. The ground is covered with snow, and there are icy patches, and, well, I just don't want you to do it."

"I'm fine. What's a little snow? Now, Gladys, don't you worry. Just get that coffee on in the morning."

The next morning Mom and I stood by her kitchen window. Mom was afraid she'd see her friend and afraid she wouldn't.

"Lillian shouldn't be out in this," she fretted, as the wind whipped past the house.

Mom's bent and arthritis-damaged body shivered with a frisson of fear as she saw the figure swathed in a heavy winter coat, wool scarf wound around her head, and big heavy mittens clutching a plastic grocery sack filled with mail.

We watched Lillian place one foot in front of the other, then struggle to do it again. She'd stop every couple of steps, bend and press forward, head down against the wind. Slowly she traveled up the alley's incline and into Mom's yard, past the little cement-block garage and into the grassy area, which was now covered with almost a foot of snow.

Lillian turned her face toward the kitchen window and saw her friend peering out. She smiled. Suddenly, she dropped the mail bag and flung her arms wide. She fell backward onto the ground.

"My God, she's fallen! I've got to help her!" Mom panicked, cursed her walker for keeping her from her friend, and sent me rushing to the back door.

She looked out of the window and yelled and motioned me to look. Tears mingled with laughter as we watched Lillian flap her arms and legs, producing a perfect snow angel.

Mom crept out of the kitchen, slowly moved her walker across the back porch and out into the yard. I ran ahead to help Lillian up and dust the snow off.

Lillian saw Mom and shouted, "You stay right there, missy! Don't you come out here!"

She laughed as Mom yelled, "You scared me half to death! Get in here and get warm."

In the doorway, they grasped each other in a hug that death could not defy. They clung to each other for another six months before Lillian slipped away.

Now, Mom makes coffee for her son, the neighbor man, and the woman down the street as they take turns bringing her mail. Someone inevitably mentions Lillian's snow angel.

Mom always smiles and nods.

Recently she said, "You know, Lillian always thanked me for being her friend, for introducing her to people and including her. But she was the one who gave me so much more."

I smiled, remembering Lillian, who always had something nice to say.

Mom continued. "She gave me a reason to get up every morning. Every morning."

Again she paused, looked out of the window to where Lillian had made the snow angel.

"I never knew what a real friend was, until she came to my house. . . . Wasn't that snow angel something?"

—*Dawn Goldsmith*

Gotta Keep Paddling

"Paddle, Norma!" he shouted.

"I'm paddling!"

"Harder!"

It was the toughest day so far, a day of grueling portages over muddy paths and flooded rocks. Twice, the weight of my sixty-pound Duluth pack had pulled me over backward. I'd waited, like a turtle on its back, for someone to stand me up.

Now, we had one stretch of white water to navigate and, soon, we'd be at our campsite. Or would we? Each attempt failed. We'd get a good start, paddle like crazy, and then lose momentum as the current swept us back to where we'd begun. Cold rain pelted our faces as we tried yet again.

"Paddle," he yelled again. "Harder!"

"I can't."

"One more time. If we don't make it, we'll portage."

Jack had found the right button. I paddled harder. I'd lost my gloves early on. My hands were chapped and cold. Each labored stroke brought increased pain as muscles unaccustomed to that kind of abuse counterattacked.

Why had no one thought to put backrests on canoe seats? Was my back the first to notice the omission? No time to think about that now. Gotta keep paddling. Force the paddle through the hostile water. Can't slow down. Plunge the paddle in the water. Make a J. Lift it out. Again. Don't hit the rocks. One more time. Gotta keep paddling.

"Keep it up!"

We paddled with a vengeance in one final push, and then the strokes became less frenzied. The water surrendered. All the pain and exhaustion were forgotten. We did it! My spirits soared.

Fifteen months earlier, I had suffered a stroke. Though my physical recovery was nearly complete, I was still shattered emotionally. *Strokes don't happen to young people,* I'd thought, *so that means I'm old, finished.* Then I lost my job. Any remaining self-esteem had plummeted in the dehumanizing ritual of the job search.

Being unemployed, recuperating from a stroke, and on the far side of forty aren't optimal job-seeking conditions. My left side still felt simultaneously numb and tingly. I'd concluded, falsely, that my speech was noticeably impaired and believed the residual facial weakness more visible than it actually was. So, I spoke only when questioned, answered those questions with as few words as possible, and refrained from smiling.

Some truths emerged. In a job market skewed in the employer's favor, older women are overlooked first. "Not getting older, getting better" is valid only when it can be communicated, and my emotional baggage had rendered me incapable of delivering the message. I'd found temporary work, but now it was time to return to the real world. Something had to be done.

Armed with outdoor experience in beach walking and bike riding on suburban sidewalks, I enrolled in an Outward Bound canoeing course. Paddling would be easy once I learned the technique, I'd reasoned. By the time I'd found out what *portage* meant, it was too late. They'd cashed my check.

On a Sunday afternoon, we met at the Duluth International Airport and boarded the Outward Bound van for the drive north to Ely, Minnesota, site of the Outward Bound school base. Though late May, it was rainy and quite chilly. Some chatted; others napped or read. I stared out the window, mesmerized by the rain and persistent drone of an inner voice: *What have you gotten yourself into?*

We'd gathered on the wet grass at the lakefront: four men, four women, and two instructors, both women. Our first order of business was a swim evaluation. No, there was no indoor heated pool. It was taking place right there, in the lake. I had read that a basic tenet of Outward Bound is "Dunk em and dry em." As I quickly learned, they don't limit that practice to fair weather.

Fully clothed, I got into a canoe with Jude, my partner. She looked resolute. Delaying the inevitable would not be an option. We rocked once in each direction, then capsized. Following instructions, we removed our shoes and socks, turned the canoe over, and swam the requisite distance, both with and then without the canoe. Finally, and most difficult, we climbed back in. My last thought before the indescribable shock of the icy water was how easy it is to tip a canoe. My first thought after changing into dry clothing, including polypropylene long johns, was that under no circumstances did I ever want to experience anything remotely like that again.

Geographically, we represented both coasts, the Midwest, and the Southwest. One man was older than my forty-six years, but a foot taller, seventy-five pounds heavier, and an experienced outdoorsman. The other men included a lawyer, a teacher, and an engineer. Among the women were an oil-company supervisor, a manager giving up that career to enter dental school, and me, zip. How could I not feel insecure among all that talent? Then I remembered: It was insecurity that had led me here.

Rounding out the women was a fellow munchkin. She matched my five-foot-two-inch, 105-pound frame but was fifteen years younger and full of the zest I'd lost of late. The instructors were equally impressive and exuded that special confidence born of competence. One, a Minnesota native, considered the Boundary Waters Canoe Area we would be traveling to be part of her extended backyard. We were in good hands.

Boot camp activities occupied the next day. We scaled a twelve-foot wall. The trust fall was just what the name implied; I stood on the edge of a rock, held my body rigid, and fell over backward, trusting the others to catch me. Considerably easier said than done. The object? To foster team problem-solving, reliance on one another, and confidence in the face of perceived danger. *Danger?*

One of the few exercises involving no rain, pain, or heart-stopping fear was pairing off and naming the things we would do if there were no obstacles. Our partner recorded our words in our journals. Topping my list was traveling in Alaska for six months and becoming a photojournalist for *National Geographic*. My recurring themes were writing, travel, and photography. It seemed those pages contained the ghost of someone I'd once known and lost track of. I missed that person and vowed to get back in touch.

A major component of Outward Bound is the

twenty-four-hour solo, a time of reflection and solitude. I was paddled to my spot after lunch on Thursday. I had a sleeping bag, ground pad, plastic tarp, my journal, and a whistle to blow in an emergency. I watched the canoe leave. I was alone. My hand rose instinctively to the whistle I wore around my neck. Softly, I blew it, only once and only to make sure it worked . . . just in case.

A chipmunk perched on the rain pants I'd draped over a rock. We studied each other. Angry clouds gathered. Using the tarp, fallen branches, and my shoelaces, I constructed my shelter. Large drops were falling before I'd tied the last knot. The chipmunk was gone. He probably thought it best not to hang out with an amateur.

With nothing else to do, I crawled in the sleeping bag and waited for the rain to stop. It didn't. Sporadic all week, it now fell in earnest. I got out my journal but immediately broke the point on the pencil.

This solo should have been enriching; the weather had turned it into another endurance contest. I coped by thinking of something else, like those Victorian brides who were told, "Close your eyes and think of England." Playing games helped, like thinking of song titles starting with each letter of the alphabet. Skipping X and Z was allowed. My game, my rules. So went the afternoon.

There was no improvement as day turned to

night. I woke often with the tarp inches from my face, weighted down by an accumulation of the incessant rain. Each time I emptied it, my frustration rose. Ultimately it turned to anger. "Enough!" I shouted heavenward. "Turn it off!" After that, it rained harder.

Though I was sure it never would, the long night ended. Upon waking, I stretched, immediately remembering why I was curled into a tight ball: The bottom of my sleeping bag was soaked, and the ground was covered with white slush—the rain had turned to snow. In the white stillness, I reflected on all that had happened.

Throughout the week, both instructors had reminded me that everyone was willing to help, but it was up to me to make my needs known. I found this difficult, if not impossible. When I told my story the first night, I received positive feedback. But later, I wondered: *What do they think of me now?* I'd been acutely aware of being unable to carry the heaviest packs or to balance a canoe on my shoulders and walk at the same time.

Now it struck me, considering my age and size, maybe I had done everything that was expected of me—or more. And maybe having had a stroke had little, if anything, to do with what I could or couldn't do.

That out of the way, I could focus on the high points. Like the time we stood looking at a varnished canoe paddle hanging decoratively on a wall.

"They should award that to you in recognition of your effort," Bob, the lawyer, had said.

Toni, an instructor, told me of an exhausted fellow student who had persevered, saying, "If she can do this, so can I."

My eyelids stung as their words danced through my head. I'm not a Pollyanna. If my illness was a blessing, it's one I could well have done without. In my opinion, people who run around chirping about lemonade haven't had to deal with many lemons of their own. The tears that fell freely now were not of self-pity, but of an awakening sense of self-worth. I'd kept relatively warm and relatively dry. And I hadn't blown the whistle.

A ship leaving the safety of the harbor for the open sea is said to be outward bound. We all create safe harbors for ourselves and only in leaving them are we truly challenged.

My self-doubt may return, but it will never again immobilize me. I'll get a job. And I'll dust off my camera and sharpen some pencils. In those last few days, I'd discovered that when the chips are down, I can paddle with the best of them.

—Norma Lewis

"Gotta Keep Paddling" was first published in New Woman magazine, November, 1989, under the byline Norma Harris.

The Last Long
Wave Good-bye

Alec O'Donnell was a short, stubby Ulsterman of indeterminate years. His legs were slightly bowed; he wore a shock of thick, black hair under his tweed cap, and on his face and tongue a brogue as thick as shoe soles.

My grandfather Harry was a tall, skinny Englishman not long out of the Cheddar Hills. His huge, knotted milker's hands hung out below the rolled sleeves of his blue chambray shirts; his English upper lip covered a drawling Somerset accent—his name was "Hawry," he said—and under his fedora, his haircut was regularly committed with a bowl.

My most persistent memory is of them sitting together at evening on my grandparents' front porch till the sun went down and the coyotes started to yip in the woodlot back of the house. They were talking, of course—always talking—sometimes so intently they couldn't interrupt even to say good night.

Eventually, heads down, hands shoved deep in their overall pockets, they strolled down the long tree-lined drive, cut across the pasture past the swamp and through the gate into Alec's yard, where they stood talking another hour or so in the yellow cone of the high barn light—and then they'd stroll back again. Some nights they made the trip three or four times before parting company.

Back on his own porch, each man would turn and wave to the other—one of those high, open-handed, long-distance waves a man gives only, trustingly, to his favorite brother. Then each would go into his own house, blink the kitchen light, and go to bed.

On a fine summer morning the year I was eight, Grandfather took me with him to pay a call at O'Donnell's house. It was early, and the dew was thick as fairy gems spilled on the grass; no one else was awake. My bare feet trotting to keep up with his big booted ones, we walked down the lane, across the pasture, and through the gate at the foot of O'Donnell's garden.

"Hello, the house," Grandfather called, and the barn door opened.

Alec O'Donnell stood there in his barn boots, his battered tweed cap jammed down around his ears. "Harry!" he called back joyfully, as if it had been years. "Ye coome visitin."

After a tour round the yard and barns, Alec led the way through his back door into the kitchen, a bare wood room occupied by a black cookstove, a plank table, two mismatched wooden chairs, and an upended coal scuttle.

I have no way of reckoning how long a time went by as I sat in privileged company with those men, listening to their talk, slurping hot tea from my saucer, but the sun went round from the east window to the south before Grandfather and I walked home.

Intense friendships—even those less enriched by proximity and goodwill, and less challenged by extremes of politics and temper and religion—are not easy to maintain. There were worms, I suppose, even in the good brown soil of Paradise. That summer morning may have been the last of the good times.

Alec was, no doubt, a peculiar man. An Irishman living alone by choice, he never really left "the ould sod," and spent a great deal of time writing and reading letters from "home." I remember my parents discussing with astonishment this fast friendship between a raging Ulsterman and an Englishman still loyal to the queen.

The O'Donnell place was pretty, the neighbors allowed, but not in any kind of tidy, white-fenced American farm kind of way. Alec had built his small, unpainted shake house on a slight rise at the foot of a hillside cherry orchard, which every spring bloomed cloud white, sheep white; against the vivid grass and the piercing sky, Mount Rainier's huge presence reigned over the landscape.

To the north was Grandfather's orchard, his clean, dry pasture and splendid new red barn; to the west, the Olympic Mountains glowed in the setting sun. Cattails, blue and yellow flags, bog lilies, skunk cabbage, and willow grew eagerly in the marshy ground between Alec's little house and the road, screening it from passersby. A gracefully curved settee formed of willow—the only thing that bog was good to grow, other than mosquitoes, my grandfather said—stood leafy, rooted, and inviting at the water's edge.

Alec was considered a failure in our little immigrant farming community. He had some chickens, a pig, a few cows. The animals kept him, but made little profit. There was a bull, too, at O'Donnell's—a glossy black angus as compact and well muscled as its master—a bull we kids enjoyed baiting to draw it away from the Irishman's weedy orchard. Because of that bull, O'Donnell's apples were irresistible, and more than once we just escaped the impact of its short, gleaming horns ramming into the red board fence.

Aside from its periodic duties with Alec's cows and Grandfather's heifers, the bull had little else to do. Our efforts to outwit him, we told each other, were in the way of benevolent exercise, though Alec did not agree. When the fence finally fell over, we were required to replace it, a job Grandfather supervised, muttering under his breath.

Grandfather had tried for years to convince his neighbor to get rid of the bull, which he considered to be dangerous, ill-tempered, and unnecessary. He also urged Alec to give up digging ditches by hand and to drain the swamp, instead—but his suggestions only made the Irishman angry.

How else if not with ditches, Alec demanded, was he to drain his fields to make them usable? Without his bog he'd be even more homesick than he already was—and the bull, it seemed, in addition to servicing the neighborhood cows, was necessary to Alec's Northern Irish pride in some way only a bone-headed, stone-hearted Englishman could fail to understand.

When Alec fell ill in the fall of 1965 and the apples in his orchard fermented on the ground instead of elsewhere, the bull became quite inebriated. He broke through the fence, got mired in the bog, and lay there all night bellowing like Judgment, till Grandfather came with his nightshirt tucked into his bib overalls and winched him out with a hand block and tackle.

But Alec felt sure, in the depths of his impetuous and decidedly unmechanical Irish soul, that Grandfather's rescue had been the near death of his prize bull.

The argument that ensued was both vicious and sad.

"Ye gully!" O'Donnell roared.

Grandfather took his hands off the block and stood, propping his stiff back with his hands. "You're an ungrateful man, Alec O'Donnell," he said. Jerking his head at me to come away, he walked up the hill toward home, leaving Alec to hop and rage like an angry leprechaun, shouting Gaelic curses at our departing backs.

Thanksgiving came, then Christmas, but Alec's merry presence did not grace our holidays.

When spring came, Grandfather made his annual trip to the feed and seed, where the men of the area gathered to choose, sharpen, and rehandle their garden implements. Grandfather joined them, talking quietly, testing shovels and rakes for balance and heft, ringing choice hoes on the feed barn's cool cement floor.

The subject of their conversation, as it had been increasingly of late, was Alec O'Donnell and his sad fortunes, which the men worried might spread. Alec had been the first in the community to come down with a new strain of Spanish flu, and recalling that the epidemic of 1918 had killed so many, they were scared. "It's that swamp." Krause stuck out his famous iron chin. "We should drain it for him, if he won't."

Such talk was not new, and I left them, but did not miss O'Donnell's entrance—or my grandfather's sudden, stiff-necked response. "Come away, now," he said to me. Reluctantly, I followed him out the door.

Alec recovered, but never regained his former strength and good humor. Nor did he and my grandfather resume their old friendship. That, I knew, had more to do with the wounded bull than with the devastation brought by flu.

By Christmas of 1966, the virus had swept through our community like fire in a stubbled field and then away to cause grief in some other place. It wasn't much of a holiday, and once again, Alec O'Donnell was missing from my grandparents' table.

The new year, too, came and went with no puckish Alec to first-foot it, ducking and smiling, capering in through our back door and out the front to bring us luck. It was that, I think, that caused my grandmother to urge a truce.

"It's almost the new year, Harry. We've come through it all right, now let bygones be bygones." She stood on tiptoe to plant a kiss on Grandfather's weathered cheek, and I was suddenly aware that my round, red-headed little grandma must once have been very pretty indeed.

"Go now," she urged him, patting his shoulder. "There are twelve days to Christmas, and they're not all gone. Friendship's a gift that won't dent your pocketbook." So Grandfather took up his cap and went.

I watched him trace the familiar path across the field, past the swamp, where he hesitated, then up through the orchard, straight to Alec O'Donnell's door—and back again. "Slammed the door in my face," he railed at Grandma Kate. "I'm damned if I'll ever speak to him again."

Still, when Alec's health failed him again, Grandfather set aside the enmity between them. He took his old friend on the half-day drive to town, first to the doctor, then the hospital. He grumbled about neglected farmwork and wasted time, but he visited Alec there once a week till, months later, he bore him home again, stubble-faced, pale, and scrawny.

Grandfather installed Alec in his own sagging bed in his own dusty front parlor and walked over several times a day—always going formally, the long way round by the road—to make sure the sick man's needs were met. It was clear, each time I went along, that they did not speak—at least, not directly.

"Tell the old coot he needn't stir his bones, I can do for meself," O'Donnell crabbed at me.

"You're bull-headed as ever," Grandfather retorted, slamming down a mug of tea just far enough away so the sick man would have to reach.

Years later, long after I was grown and Alec O'Donnell had been reduced from his lowland farm to one of four beds in a nursing home ward, I dropped by on my lunch hour to bring him a stack of National Geographic magazines and a sheaf of blue and yellow iris—and found Grandfather there. He had draped his cantankerous neighbor in an extra sheet, cranked him up in his bed, and was shaving him with the straight razor Alec once kept on the shelf in his tidy bachelor kitchen.

Making the same soothing throat noises he used to quiet his beasts, Grandfather applied hot towels to Alec's sad and angry face. He brushed on thick lather, stropped the razor and applied it skillfully, maneuvering around the large, delicate, elfin ears; across wrinkles deep as drainage ditches; under bagged eyes and sagging chin.

Three other old men watched intently: one standing by the window in a hospital gown and paper slippers, two others peering rheumy-eyed from under their covers. None of them noticed me, and I stood there in the doorway, remembering the mired Black Angus bull.

But then—it was a small moment, one I nearly missed—Alec O'Donnell, Irish to the soul, laid his weary head, deliberate, trusting, into my grandfather's gentle hold.

So I took my flowers and magazines, and went away tear-struck and smiling, remembering two huge hands raised in long greeting at twilight across an unproductive bog . . . and the kitchen light signal, a quicksilver message sent between two silent, distant stars.

—*Marjorie Rommel*

Begin Again

I stared at Leonard, this man I had married to fill Richard's place, to be the replacement part that would make me whole again. I didn't want to think of Richard then, but his question, a challenge really, had dumbfounded me:

"Didn't Richard's death teach you anything?"

Where had that come from?

Leonard's eyes refused to break contact. They held me. Warm blue eyes. Richard's had been a deep velvety brown. Strong eyes, which crinkled and went soft when he smiled. Leonard's hair clung close to his head in tiny tight curls, a brownish slate on its way to gray. Richard's hair had been straight and thick, jet-black until cancer and chemo played tug-of-war and pulled it all away. How had I fused these two men together in my head? I'd never stopped to notice before how unlike they were.

Was I Leonard's Janet? Did he, too, see her when he looked at me, held me, loved me? Had he ever noticed how dissimilar my Lady Clairol brown bob was from her beauty parlor frosting? From photographs, I had decided she, too, was small-boned and rounded, like me, not fat but lightly padded. My eyes are green, and hers were . . . I don't know; the pictures don't show me. What color were Janet's eyes?

Eyes. Leonard's were still watching me, waiting for his answer.

Yes, Leonard, Richard's death taught me many things, private things I can't voice, not yet. It taught me no amount of denial could make bad things go away. It taught me we'd wasted too many hours being irritated, arguing over things that weren't worth a damn. I'd ignore every one of them now, embrace every quirk or unreasonableness to have him back. Too late. I learned that "away forever" never sinks in. Like when the sight of a new biography of Abraham Lincoln in the bookstore window spiraled me toward the entrance, until I felt the sting, like a slap across my face, that told me I couldn't surprise him with my find of a new book about his favorite historic character. Not then. Not ever. Never.

Yes, I knew death. I'd learned its lessons. Why did Leonard ask me that? Why then? We'd been discussing my retirement. I was eligible that June. He wanted me to quit. I planned to work another five years, until I was sixty-five. I hadn't had a full career at sixty, as he had. I had waited until my children were teenagers before, at forty-five, I'd gone back to teaching. I wanted to work some more, to round out my total to twenty years. Why not?

So I challenged Leonard's gaze—green eyes could grip as well as blue—as we sat in the overfurnished living room, cluttered with our combined possessions. His lime-green couches encircled my oversized mahogany coffee table. My blue-green upholstered chairs that clashed with the couches lurked in corners. His too-large oak entertainment center, backed against a wall, glared at my classic seascapes beside his Japanese prints. We'd comingled everything, as we'd done with our mates past and present. He absentmindedly called me Janet, and I answered, because I as often called him Richard. Nothing matched, but we blended everything to make it work for us. We needed the familiar.

"Janet and I had planned to move to Laguna Beach when I retired. She didn't live long enough," he said.

"Cape Cod was our choice. We spent summers there when we lived back East," I answered.

"We wanted to have time for classes, all kinds of classes. Janet loved music. I wanted to do pottery."

"Richard and I dreamed of traveling."

"We could do both," Leonard suggested. "I like to travel."

So that's where the question came from. He thought he could entice me to see it his way, but I saw through it. Yet, he'd pushed the buttons, and I wanted my lost dreams back. I was going to say, *Just think, in five years we'll have all the time in the world to do whatever we want,* but he spoke first.

"None of us knows when the shoe will drop. We should play while we can."

My logic blew away. I retired. I didn't miss the school, my office, my job, and its parade of people and impossible tasks, after all. We pulled up stakes and headed for the Seattle area, which I had pegged as a future home someday. We were free. We built a new identity in a new community. We were a pair, at last. We traveled to all my planned places and others I'd not dreamed of. We tried salmon fishing from our shared seventeen-foot Bayliner. We hit the road, Winnebago style. I learned to do things I never knew I could handle. Everything was new. Everything was fun. We were young again beneath our wrinkles.

Until the cancer. The surgeon said we caught it in time, though it cost Leonard a third of his right lung. No matter. A year later, he ran the same ten-kilometer race we'd done the month before his surgery. His time wasn't as good and he wheezed, but he still beat me, as always. Beat me and the cancer, we'd thought.

Three years later, while tramping around Australia,

he commented that something was wrong with his gait; he'd probably have to have surgery on his knee when we got home. It wasn't a cause for concern. He'd done the other knee years earlier. Not unusual for a runner, he told me. We headed on to New Zealand.

In Auckland, he started to limp. In Dunedin, we bought a cane. By Christchurch, I was handling the luggage. It was time to go home.

"It's not your knee," the doctor said. "I want an MRI of your head."

Brain tumor. Malignant. Pathology report: brain tumor, lung cancer cells. MRI of the spine. Inoperable tumors. Radiation. When lung cancer metastasizes to multiple parts of the body, figure six months. The oncologist suggested hospice.

He died at home. I was sixty-four, one year short of my originally planned retirement age. There would have been no play time, no partner to travel with, no daring a new life in a new community, all our adventures lost. Four years of pure kid-again fun, saved by an earlier-than-planned retirement.

Yes, Leonard, you were right. And yes, Richard's death taught me a lot. But your death taught me more. You taught me to live in the moment and to savor life. I've learned I can go on without you, and I value my days for all of us.

—*Marcia Rudoff*

Warm Hearts in a Cold Winter

The calendar read December 15. It had been one of the hardest months of my life, and I didn't feel much like getting out of bed that morning. The sound of three sets of small feet thundering outside my bedroom left me little choice.

"Mama, we're hungry! Mama, come on! Time to get up, Mama!"

The scurrying feet disappeared down the stairs, and I knew I'd better hurry if I was going to salvage my house.

My husband Don had left for work hours before, leaving me the luxury of sleeping in until then. I dragged myself out of bed. Because I was eight months pregnant, it took great time and effort just to get to my feet, let alone get dressed. So I pulled on my old maroon robe and hurried to the kitchen as fast as my lumbering body could move. On my way, I heard the echoes of croupy coughs, a remnant from the family illness we were trying unsuccessfully to discard.

When I reached the kitchen, I saw three runny-nosed children standing with the fridge door open, looking for something for breakfast. Just as I got them all situated with bowls of cold cereal and had slumped down into a chair, the phone rang.

"Mrs. Gore?" a husky voice with a heavy German accent asked.

"Yes."

"This is Mr. Schreiber, your landlord."

I wondered why he was calling first thing in the morning. I was certain he had received our rent.

"I just wanted to let you know that the house has sold, and you have to be moved out by January fifth."

"But that only gives us three weeks to find another place," I objected.

"I'm sorry, Mrs. Gore, there's not a thing I can do about it. That's when the buyers want to close. The date is already set. You've got to be out by then."

As I hung up the phone, my mind began to spin at the tasks that loomed ahead. It sent me into a coughing fit.

"Mama, are you all right?" my three-year-old daughter asked.

"Yes, honey. Everything is fine," I reassured her, once I'd stopped coughing, even though I was not so sure of it myself.

When my husband, Don, returned home from work late that night, I broke the news to him.

"How can they expect us to be out in three weeks?" I asked. "It's just not right. Christmas is only a week and a half away, and with all of us being so sick lately, I've had almost no chance to shop."

"I don't see as we have much choice, Kathy. You'll just have to make phone calls during the day, and I'll go looking for a place after I get off work."

For the next two and a half weeks, I made phone calls during the day and Don went house-hunting in the evening.

Our coughing and fevers hung on all through the holiday season. At times, I worried that my coughing fits would send me into labor. I had never felt so sick, not even in the early months of morning sickness. What was worse was that the children and Don were also plagued with it. Christmas was cold and bleak. Instead of our usual tradition of opening gifts and going to the grandparents' homes to visit and enjoy treats reserved only for the holiday, on that Christmas Day we opened gifts and slept away most of the day, not feeling well enough to even enjoy our own presents.

The holidays came and left, and moving day arrived. It was the first time I had even set foot inside our new home. Both my mother and Don's mother were worried about me overdoing it, so they made to help clean the new house and to finish packing after. Still, I pushed myself to my limits, determined the house would be clean when we moved in. Every half hour or so, I had to lie down on the floor to catch my breath and to stop a coughing spasm, only to have it begin again a few minutes later.

The children, at least, seemed to be feeling much better. They ran through the house exploring all the possibilities their new house held. They searched out every new hiding place and wore trails in the carpet. By three in the afternoon, we were ready to return to the old house to finish packing.

"I'm sorry I can't help you pack, Kathy," my mother-in-law apologized, giving me a comforting hug. "I just phoned home, and Jon is really sick. I need to go and take care of him. Will you be okay?"

"Sure." I pasted on a smile, but my heart sank. "I'm sure we'll be able to handle it. You go on home and take care of things there."

My mother gave me a hug good-bye as well.

"I'll try to come by later tonight, dear."

After an hour or so of packing, I began to fix dinner and the phone rang.

"I'm on my way home from work," Don apologized. "I'm sorry I'm so late getting off, but we poured cement today, and since I'm the only one that can operate the crane, there was no way I could leave early. How are things going?"

I reported with some satisfaction that the new house was clean, but that I was completely exhausted.

Don reminded me, "You do remember that some of the men from church will be there at six to help us move . . .?"

I glanced at my watch; it was already five o'clock!

"I thought they were coming at seven," I said. "I don't know how I'll get everything else packed in an hour. I've been moving at a snail's pace all day, and my head is ready to explode."

"I know, honey. Just do the best you can. I'll be home in twenty minutes to help."

All too soon, six o'clock arrived, and so did our moving help. The winter's chill moved inside the house as furniture was carried out. In a matter of minutes, the inside temperature dropped to below freezing. Don was busy coordinating the men who had come to help, while I packed, trying to keep ahead of them. I put the children in an upstairs bedroom to keep them warm, hoping they would find something to play with. Unfortunately, since all of their toys were packed away, soon all three were crying from both the cold and boredom.

The phone rang at six-fifteen. It was my mother. As she began to talk, I glanced across the kitchen and noticed that one of the men helping us move was sitting at the table writing in a tablet.

"I'm sorry, I'm not going to be able to help you pack," my mother said. "When I got home, I found your brother, Ray, had come home sick. He hasn't had a thing to eat. I can't come back tonight. Will you be all right?"

Of course I wasn't all right. I had never felt so not all right and alone in all my life. I turned my head away to hide my tears. Steadying my shaky voice, I told my mom that we would be fine.

When I hung up, I felt our friend's eyes upon me. "Are you okay?" he asked.

All I could do was nod my head yes.

I was so embarrassed—embarrassed at my tears, embarrassed at my messy house that I hadn't felt well enough to clean for weeks, embarrassed at my children who were screaming from the upstairs bedroom. Overwhelmed by it all, I left the room and went to the rescue of my three little children, praying that somehow I might be rescued. I closed the bedroom door, sat on the floor, and cried with my children.

"I just can't do it," I wept. "What am I supposed to do?"

About fifteen minutes later, after I'd regained my composure, I left the bedroom to face the impossible chore before me. To my surprise, my house was a bustle of activity. Several women were in the kitchen cleaning; one had even started to attack the oven, a task worse than death. Another whisked my crying children away to her warm house, assuring me not to worry about a thing; she would put them to bed, and when we were all finished, we could come get them.

Soon after, the trucks were loaded with furniture. Don suggested that I ride along to the new house so that I could show them where everything went. As soon as the beds were unloaded, they set one up for me to lie on. I was not allowed to lift another finger the rest of the night.

Our good neighbors cleaned the other house from the uppermost walls down to the cobweb-covered basement. Then they unpacked several of the kitchen boxes and food, so that the next morning could begin without catastrophe. When they were finished, they disappeared into the night, not even waiting for a thank-you. I never saw most of those good Samaritans again; I don't even remember most of their names. But I do remember the love they showed me on a cold winter night, at a time in my life when I needed it most.

Ten days later, on January 15, I gave birth to our fourth child, Joshua. All settled in, with the weeks of illness and chaos finally passed, we welcomed our new baby into a peaceful, comfortable home.

Recently, I was asked to speak at Joshua's Boy Scout Eagle Court of Honor ceremony. I recounted how eighteen years earlier a man had seen a neighbor in distress. He could have just ignored her troubles, but he didn't. He involved other neighbors and lifted a burden from her shoulders that was too heavy for her to bear, blessing her in a way she was never able to reciprocate.

I told Joshua that, instead, I have tried to repay that man's kindness by doing similar things for others over the years. My plea to Joshua was that he might follow his example and become the kind of man who sees the need in others and reaches out to help. I can't think of a better tribute to that honorable man whose generosity warmed my heart so many years ago.

—Kathryn Gore

For Sura, Who Claimed
Her Need to Be Touched

The sweltering air was still cooler than that of the barren landscape, where a heat haze shimmered beyond the bus windows. I was wedged tightly between country folk returning home from the Souk, the city market. Women in *bourkas* or heavy black overcoats attempted to deal with lively children, who, in turn, teased the hens and goats on board. The animals and birds had their legs tethered and were upset and noisy, creating bedlam.

The men, all in traditional Arabic dress, by and large ignored the disorder except to give an occasional sharp reprimand. Mostly, they chatted among themselves and smoked. The fumes of hash were pungent, and I felt heady as I eyed flies circling dazedly around my face or settling on me to suck up my sweat. Two old men at the back drew on a bubbling *hookah*, cocooned in their own contentment.

Baskets of ripe fruit, vegetables, and market purchases were squeezed in among the mass of passengers, and served to stabilize the chaotic cargo as we were jolted along. I was bewitched by the exotic scene, engrossed by my fellow travelers.

From where I stood, I could see that the hood of the bus was tied together with frayed string, reinforced with lengths of wire, and I wondered a little anxiously what would happen if we did not make it to our destination safely. I did not even know the language to negotiate my way back to the city. My friends knew I had planned this trip and would know where to search, but much could happen to a Canadian woman traveling alone in the Middle East in 1974.

It was in this fashion that I journeyed to the hospital where Sura came into my life.

The sun-battered building was on the edge of the desert, and the first thing I noticed when I entered was the offensive smell. It was inescapable and immediately saturated my entire body, hair, and clothes. I found myself breathing shallowly in defense.

I asked one of the staff who understood English for a drink of water and was told that I may have one glass, but there was very little and I must make it last. When I became more familiar with the living conditions on the wards, I saw that patients nursed their glass for hours, restricting themselves to small sips from time to time. I was moved when many offered to share theirs with me, even though they had never met me before and I was clearly a foreigner. My throat soon became parched, and my longing for a drink made me appreciate the lakes of my homeland in a way I had never given thought to before.

Personal hygiene, too, was extraordinarily challenging. Because of the scarcity of water, toilets often filled up and the contents overflowed to the surrounding floors and hallways. This unsanitary environment was difficult to keep under control and undermined morale.

As I could not speak Arabic, the only way I could communicate with patients was by gesture and touch. Often, though, this was actually a benefit. Many of the patients were refugees who had lost their homes, belongings, and most of their clothes in the political disturbance that beset their country. Worse, a number were also survivors who had seen family members killed. My human presence was an essential; my words much less relevant.

I made my way from bed to bed, caressing hands, stroking hair, putting as much as I could muster into a smile, and offering a dab of cologne to refresh fevered skin. When I came to babies, I gazed into their eyes and tickled tummies to force a response, knowing that the lack of stimulation might result in loss of normal growth and even lead to death.

When I reached Sura's bedside, I was exhausted from the long hours and confused by the repeated exposure to traumatized lives.

I found her lying flat on her back under a thin sheet, her breath barely raising its worn fabric. She had no pillow, and her hair was matted and neglected, slick with sweat. She was moaning weakly. She had been wounded in the face by an exploding shell.

Dressings were in short supply, and her infected sores had been left open to the air in the hope that they would crust over and dry out. The areas where they oozed pus were a seething mass of black flies and other insects, some sucking on the deteriorating flesh, others hovering to take their turn. She tried from time to time to brush them off, but had not the strength to raise her hands effectively. I attempted to shoo them away, but they simply slipped aside on the currents of air my efforts created and soon returned to her wounds. I felt frustrated and powerless.

She first became aware of my presence when she felt the cool breeze as I waved away the flies. She opened her eyes curiously to see what was happening. Her lips were too cracked to smile easily, but her expression quickened as if she knew me. She murmured something I could not catch, although I thought I heard the word "Allah." Most of the patients were devout Muslims, who constantly expressed praise in Allah's name.

I bent closer, wondering how I could best help her, and as I did so, she made a supreme effort to reach my face, pulled my head down, and kissed me full on the lips.

Her action so took me by surprise that I failed to react against it and thereby remained open to feeling fully the authenticity of her need. Normally, I am sure that I would have gagged at the feel of the infection against my mouth, but instead I was awed.

Her need for human touch was so great that I understood, not just intellectually but with my entire body, the immensity of her risk and the trust she'd placed in me. A compassion and gratitude that seemed much greater than my capacity to feel took hold of me. I was aware of myself and of Sura, not so much as individuals, but as beings caught up in a wider human field that is usually outside most people's consciousness. Tears brimmed between us, but not of sorrow. We both understood, through the human and deeply spiritual quality of the encounter, a bond that made the differences between us irrelevant.

Although there was no need for words at the time, I would like to say now, "Thank you, Sura. Your trust of me transformed my life and has remained one of my most precious gifts. I know for certain that in some way you can hear me."

—*Barbara Whitby*

 Recipe for Life

Father Mike was short, bald, round, and quintessentially Italian. He was sent to our parish, which is near a large medical center, to die. Instead, his cancer went into remission, and he renewed and revitalized our church family.

Father Mike was a people person. He had an uncanny ability to focus entirely on whoever was his partner in conversation, vitally interested in the person and what was being said. Many priests, understandably, seek the peace and solitude of the rectory after parish events. Not Father Mike.

"What are you doing afterward?" he would ask us, instead.

So, he often wound up at our home and quickly became a part of our family.

He loved our Lord, his parishioners, and food. He once described heaven as his mother's house on a

Sunday afternoon, full of people, laughter, story-telling, and homemade ravioli. We felt honored when he shared his recipe for spaghetti and meatballs with us. Out the window went the bottled sauce and boxed spaghetti, and in came the delectable aroma of simmering homemade spaghetti sauce. This was not a recipe that could be hurried; it took time. But since we knew it was a favorite of his, when he visited, it frequently appeared on our table.

Father Mike brought not only the gift of delicious food to our home; he also brought wisdom. He told funny stories about his childhood, sharing lessons learned around his family's dinner table, brightening our home with his rich laughter. As he settled in comfortably, waiting for dinner, he'd encourage our teenage children to question him about faith. Waiting was never an imposition to Father Mike; it was part of the pleasure of the meal. Once, my husband was running late, and I was fretting because the guest was present, but the host was not.

"Relax," Father Mike counseled, "The sauce smells superb, and we now have time to enjoy the fragrance and each other."

A few moments later, Ted came flying in like a 747 making a crash landing.

"Slow down, my friend. The sauce is simmering. It gives us time."

It is an understatement to say that, as a parish

priest, Father Mike's time was at a premium. But knowing that sharing a meal with members of his church community was high on his priority list, we'd drop by the rectory often, issuing an invitation.

"Hey, Father Mike, want to go get Mexican food?"

His eyes would light up as he'd say, "I love Mexican (or Chinese or Italian or hamburgers)!"

On one occasion when the restaurant's service was extremely slow, I began to fidget, trying to discern the cause of the delay. "What could be taking so long?"

"Oh, but this is great! We have time to visit. I've been wanting to tell you about this new book I'm reading."

To Father Mike's delight, a delay simply meant that he could spend more time with people. I asked him how he could remain so unflappable and unhurried, when he had so many responsibilities.

"Because people are more important than tasks."

His response gave me pause. *How would my life be different if I applied that axiom?* It was food for thought. I smiled as I realized he was teaching me not only to appreciate well-seasoned, carefully prepared food for the body; he was also teaching me to appreciate gently nurtured relationships, food for my soul.

Father Mike was in his late fifties, and it surprised us when he announced he wanted to participate in the youth group activities. Ted and I sponsored the group, and we knew how much time and energy it took.

"I like being around young people. I like their enthusiasm. They keep me young. Besides," he added, eyes dancing, "Have you noticed they always have snacks when they gather?"

Father Mike's easygoing humor became a staple at our youth functions. He cheered them on at athletic events and encouraged their participation in parish liturgies. He stayed up late with them at lock-ins. He was there for them without fail and without question.

I'll never forget the time Father Mike, a New Yorker born and bred, climbed up on the back of a horse when we took our group to a dude ranch. The kids loved it, and he was pleased as punch with himself. He sat astride his mount and surveyed the world from the new perspective, his grin as wide as the Mississippi.

At another outing, one of the youth questioned Father Mike whether he didn't have more important things to do than to picnic with a bunch of crazy kids.

"This is important," he replied.

I later realized that Father Mike was demonstrating the "ministry of presence" perfectly. Just being there: That's what counts.

When his cancer returned and claimed his life within a few short weeks, I was heartbroken. I was also angry with him for leaving me. Who would I talk to? I had come to rely on his calming effect in my life, on his good humor, on his wisdom. I wanted him there, so I could make spaghetti and meatballs for him. In my grief, I pulled out the ingredients and started the process, talking to Father Mike all the while. By the time the sauce was simmering, I felt better. Food therapy? Maybe. I'm sure it was what Father Mike would have advocated.

It wasn't until many years after he'd gone home to heaven to enjoy his mother's ravioli that we discovered that many of his parishioners had special Father Mike recipes, each one different, each a "favorite" of Father Mike's. Not only had he shared himself, his counsel, his stories, his joy of life, and his terrific recipes with each of us, but he had also arranged to have his much-loved dishes on a regular basis. A sneaky one, that Father Mike!

To this day, when his spaghetti sauce bubbles gently on the back burner and the scent wafts through my home, I am comforted. Father Mike's wisdom is presented to me once again.

People are more important than tasks. Just be there. Take time. Savor the moment.

—*Nancy Baker*

The Gift of Robin

A person's soul can be found by looking into their eyes, but I didn't need to know any more about Robin's sweet soul. What I needed was an idea of what I could do for the person who does so much for everyone else. It wasn't her birthday; I just felt an overwhelming desire to let her know how much I cherish her. Does anyone do that anymore? More important, it seems to me, does anyone inspire it in others? Robin does.

Everything about her is a thrill ride. Her enthusiasm bounces as high as her disdain does at times. What remains constant is her passion for living. And for the people who are fortunate enough to have earned her love.

Years ago, on my wedding night, my groom and I had devoured the picnic she'd left in our limousine almost as ardently as we had each other. I gave birth to my son on Thanksgiving, and there through the haze of first-time motherhood was Robin with a homemade turkey dinner to go.

Then, my family moved to a new city, and she was the last person I saw as the truck pulled away. My only comfort, later that night, was to open the cooler she had given us and find cheese, fruit, bread, bottled water, and anything we might need (M&Ms) before our kitchen was set up. All that was missing was her understanding face.

So, as I prepared my kids and I to pay our first visit to her since our move, I looked forward to crawling into her nest and enjoying everything that being in her presence has to offer. It is more than good food and a beautifully warm and inviting home, it's her. But what could I bring? Could I outcook her? Could I outshop her? Could I do anything for this woman any better than she does for everyone else? I didn't think so.

My answer came when my mind's eye looked to her hands. They contradicted everything about her. Whereas she is full of energy and enthusiasm, her hands have come to look rather tired since I've known her. Where she is bright and quick, they seem to want to just slow down for a while. An idea was born.

After we swam and jumped rope, after we barbecued and ate, and gave baths and kissed and tucked in, after we prepared sixty T-shirts to tie-dye as favors for her daughter's birthday party the next day,

I told her to sit down. It was one o'clock in the morning, but I would not miss this chance to give something back to my friend of twenty-two years.

I sat next to her on the big leather sofa in their sunken family room that has an aquarium for a wall, and picked up one of her tired hands. With plenty of almond-scented massage lotion and a little bit of muscle, I slowly began the process of letting her feel how much she is appreciated.

First, I squeezed the palm of her left hand with all my might. It's funny, but you never really know how tired your hands and feet are until someone picks them up and starts rubbing them for you. I gently pulled each of her fingers, then went back and pinched the thin skin between each one.

You could see the tension lifting from her body as her skin lapped up the moisture. Not wanting to break the calm of the silence, my thoughts went to everything her hands must've done through the years, for so many other people. Her husband, her daughters, her stepchildren, her mother, and her sister, as well as a large circle of friends, always seem to let Robin be the giver. Myself included, I must add. She just makes it so easy. I was happy to be able to give something back, if only for a few ticks of a late-night clock.

—*Julie Clark Robinson*

Balance

The boy, K., reaches for the dial to change the radio station, which he has unabashedly deemed too uncool for his sixteen-year-old ears. He catches my stare at the circular scars lining his otherwise smooth arm.

In a voice that I have not heard all evening, one that is clear, yet somehow detached, he says, "Those are from my mother and her husband when they used to burn me with their cigarettes."

I shiver, despite my feeble resolve to be strong.

"But that was a long time ago," he continues, realizing his reality may be too harsh for me. His speech impediment has returned; the one I've grown accustomed to now. "I haven't seen them since they left me on Diane's doorstep. But I promised I would take care of my mom and sister, and I swear I will find them someday."

I marvel at how his sense of inherent protection has survived. I, on the other hand, cannot disguise my horror at just bearing witness to the scars on his soul, which are far more gruesome than the ones on his body. And I am speechless. Dozens of inadequate words flit through my mind as I try to phrase an apology on behalf of humanity to this boy who has known nothing but pain. I try to think of something to say to erase his terrible memories and to replace them with a vision of a happy ending I know he won't have. I try to find expressions of wisdom and sanity in a world in which he's known neither. I cannot find the words.

Instead, I put my hand on top of his and squeeze it gently, yet purposefully. I want him to feel a hand that doesn't strike, that only comforts. I let him see the tears that have gathered in my eyes, and I say, "No one has the right to do that to you, K. They can't hurt you anymore. You're safe now."

My headlights illuminate a safe harbor. This is a place you do not hear about on the news, a refuge for children not expected to survive. The woman responsible for saving hundreds of abused boys and young men who've lived there, anxiously greets us in the driveway as we return from our outing.

We are immediately welcomed by some of the other residents, eager to hear of his adventure at the hockey game. K. is a willing and proud narrator, and they are captivated by his story.

"Was he good?" Diane asks me tentatively.

"Of course he was," I answer honestly. I have never witnessed poor behavior from any of the boys in the three years since I met this amazing family.

Our conversation is brief. With twenty-two children inside needing her attention, Diane has little time for chitchat. It is time for this tireless, dedicated woman and her husband, Sandy, to begin bedtime rituals for the boys who live there.

I am in awe of her grace as I watch her walk into the house with a trail of laughing boys behind her. No one would guess that this petite, pretty woman is made of steel with a heart of pure gold.

Diane and Sandy established Attention Home more than twenty years ago. Despite its ordinary suburban appearance, miracles are performed there daily. Attention Home is a full-time residential group home that provides services and care for special needs individuals, most of whom have come there to escape some of the worst child abusers in the state of Florida.

My experience with this home has been a lesson in delicate balance. When I am around the boys of Attention Home, I must push from my mind the heinous crimes that have been committed against them, so that they can heal in an environment free of hostility and negativity. Yet, I must never forget those crimes, so that I never lose sight of how important it is that they do heal. This exercise is always brutal for the few hours I spend with them. Diane must maintain this complicated equilibrium every minute of every day.

The boys of Attention Home are graciously receptive to any love and kindness shown them, making it easy to give it generously. Looking at their sweet faces, I struggle to reconcile my feelings of anger and injustice with forgiveness and healing.

How can one forgive the parent who locked his son in a room with a dog and threw his food to him like the animal he shared his cell with? When authorities finally rescued him, the boy could not talk or walk, could only bark and crawl. But rather than focusing on the tragedy, Diane forgave so that she could turn her attention to the child. Thanks to Diane's love and care, he now speaks and walks and is a happy ten-year-old.

What does one say to the seven-year-old boy who was found foraging for food in a dumpster at 3:00 A.M., abandoned by his parents? Diane doesn't explain with words; she responds with a nurturing consistency he has never known.

As for K., I mourn both his lost childhood and his lost adulthood. The wounds inflicted on him have rendered him sixteen forever, and somehow that is not so sweet. I see him poised on the horizon between childhood and adulthood, unable to fully embrace either.

Whereas I am struck powerless by the injustice,

Diane is empowered. Whereas I am blinded by anger, her eyes are wide open to the light of solution.

She reminds me that she is not a saint. She is human and has children and grandchildren of her own. Her emotions are flawed, but she is usually able to overcome them. I know she doesn't walk on water, but she wades through it so admirably that it is a thing to behold. She gives me the courage to dive in after her.

Therein lies the profound difference between someone you can admire and someone who inspires you. I am able to help in small ways, because she shows me that acts of kindess weigh more in the life of a child. Meanwhile, the walls of Attention Home—and the heart of this loving family—continue to expand to harbor more boys in need of sanctuary and love.

The next time I visit Attention Home, I bring my son with me. K. greets me with robust hugs and takes my two-year-old from my arms as if by instinct. Anticipating resistance from my stranger-phobic toddler, I am about to make an apology so as not to hurt K.'s tender feelings, but the words stop short in my throat. I do not know what amazes me more, that my son is perfectly at ease within K.'s embrace or that K. knew he would be. It strikes me then that the elusive balance I seek is not in the shape of a horizon, but rather a circle.

—*Tracey Henry*

Why I Carry a Bobolight

"Oh, now what the heck is that?"

We'd already asked ourselves that question, or some variation of it, a hundred times that day. We would ask it probably another hundred times before we'd finished. But for the time being, our attention was riveted by the bag of oddly shaped blue thingies on the top shelf of the smaller basement storage room.

"I don't know, Dad," I said. I was ready to move on. We were sorting the stuff in my grandpa's house the day after his funeral, and we were all too raw from grief to think very clearly. "If you don't know, let's just let it go, and get back to sorting the pictures and the stuff we're sure we want to put up at auction."

My dad rattled the bag and then said slowly, "Heeey! Do you remember these? I didn't know any of them were still around."

He opened the bag and took one out. It was shaped like a pipe with a blue stem and some odd holes along the side, but instead of a bowl there was a yellow plastic sphere.

I shrugged. "I don't even know what they are, Dad."

"It's your grandpa's invention."

"What?"

Dad held the thing yellow-globe-up. "Yeah, it's for night fishing. It would rest on the water until you got a bite." He bobbed it up and down, turning it a little in midair. "There's a mercury switch inside, and when it got a good tug—not just a nibble, but an actual bite—the light would come on, and you'd know you'd snagged one."

"Grandpa was an inventor?"

"What were they called? . . . Bobbers? . . . No. . . . Bobolights! You don't remember them putting these together in the basement over on Valley Way?"

My dad reminisced about the gadget's manufacturing process for a while. When we got the dates straight, I felt better about not remembering exactly what they were. I'd been only seven or eight when they were being made. The more we talked about them, though, the more I remembered having seen them around before, not realizing what exactly it was that I had seen.

That felt appropriate for this visit back home and

for everything surrounding my grandfather's funeral. I knew my grandfather. At least, I'd thought I did. I didn't think we were much alike, but I thought I had him pretty well pegged.

Then came the discussions at the viewing and the funeral, and I learned otherwise. Oh, don't get me wrong. There weren't any shocking exposés or anything like that. What was surprising was how much of him there was.

You know how nine-tenths of an iceberg is invisible, because most of it is below the surface of the water? Well, my knowledge of Grandpa was like that. Much about him was invisible to me, but instead of the hidden part being cold and frozen, it was as warm and alive as the ten percent of him I was able to see.

I'd known my grandfather had been a Mason; I hadn't known he was a Master Mason or that he had been a member for more than fifty years. I had known he attended regularly; I didn't realize that meant another entire phalanx of friends, ranging from my grandfather's age of eighty-plus to around thirty, who would be at the funeral, and who would be weeping as hard as my family for their loss.

I had, of course, known that my grandfather had other grandchildren. I even knew he was close to them, maybe closer than he was to me, since I'd lived so far away. What I hadn't known was how much he had meant to his cousins. And to his second cousins and third cousins. And to his nieces and nephews, and to his grand-nieces and -nephews.

I had known my grandfather was fond of his neighbor Bill. My grandpa was a great storyteller, and Bill figured into some of his best stories. What I hadn't known, but should have guessed, was how important my grandpa was to Bill. He came over the day we were sorting things. He was ravaged.

"I don't know what I'm going to do," he said. "I've lived in this town for two years, and your grandfather was my closest friend."

Later I learned that in the final months, when his health had taken a turn for the better, it had looked like my grandfather would be able to come home. My mom and uncles were worried that he wouldn't be able to take care of himself. They'd voiced their concerns, and Grandpa had interrupted with, "Well, I've been thinking about that, and I'm going to ask Bill to help and pay him for his time."

Everyone was hesitant about this, because Bill worked full time and had a young child, but when he was asked, Bill said simply, "Of course."

I think Bill said "of course" so readily because, well, he was a good man, but also because my grandfather would have done the same for him. He had done the same—had plowed his drive, mowed his yard, mulched his leaves, and more, with a casual zest that downplayed just how much work and effort he was giving. How much he always gave, to everyone who'd asked and to many who hadn't.

Should I mention that Bill was black and that my grandfather was white and raised in a small farming community in southern Ohio, where racism was common? I feel like I shouldn't, because it didn't matter to him—but then I know I must, because it was one of a hundred ways in which he was special. When he'd been a foreman at Ford Motor Company, black and Hispanic workers had transferred to my grandfather's shift. Indeed, some took a pay cut to do so, and so many transferred in, that his supervisors blinked when they entered his area of the plant, because white faces were so rare there. This was in the 1960s and 1970s, in an area of Ohio where racial unrest was pretty common. When many white Americans were wincing at riots on television and civil rights agitation, my grandparents were being the only white folks invited to black social events.

When I asked him about it, my grandfather tended to wave it away, saying that it was nothing special, his insistence on treating a man fairly and judging a worker on the quality of his work and nothing else. But he had to know how rare that was. Certainly his workers did. Anybody who takes a pay cut, or works graveyard rather than day shift, or refuses a promotion in order to work for someone, says something.

That "something" wasn't about my grandfather's skill at his job. Oh, they respected him for that, too, no doubt. My grandfather could fix anything, and often did. But what they were reacting to in my grandfather was his character.

My grandfather was proud of his prowess as a worker, and this prowess was so extreme that it was easy to let it overshadow his character. I know I let it do so. I was so impressed by his work as a farmer, a machinist, a postmaster, someone who could garden, hunt, wire, paint, plaster, repair, cook, and more, that for the longest time I was afraid I didn't measure up. That I couldn't be the man my grandfather was, and that he would judge me for failing to do so.

But then came the funeral. I saw hod carriers and doctors, friends and relatives, black and white, young and old, and they all told the same kind of stories about my grandfather. And I realized that he had one last gift to give me, one that the Bobolight has come to symbolize.

To be like my grandfather, I didn't have to be my grandfather. He didn't ask that of any of the people who came to the funeral. He didn't ask that of any of the people who loved him. He asked only two things of them. He asked them to be good and to be themselves, the best that they could be. And—here's the part that still makes me cry—he trusted that these were the same thing. He believed that being me and being good were the same thing.

I have often felt swamped by life. I've felt like I was drowning, like there were forces overwhelming me and pulling me under. Like I wasn't good enough. But since my grandfather's funeral, I've felt a new clarity about being who I am. It's why I carry the Bobolight.

You see, the Bobolight didn't make my grandfather rich. He hoped it would and he'd had the technical expertise to make a great night-fishing light, but not the marketing savvy to make a bundle of cash selling them. But he kept those lights for more than twenty years, because they were something he'd made and he was proud of them.

Do you know what is even more amazing? I found a stash of newspaper clippings and mementos of achievements I'd obtained throughout my life and of other people who were important to him, carefully covered in plastic and kept up where Grandpa could see them. Meanwhile, he stored his invention out of sight in the basement. He was more proud of his loved ones than of his own accomplishments.

Therein lies the brilliance of the Bobolight. The Bobolight goes on when you've got a real opportunity that you can't see. It helps you separate the nibbles— the false bites—from the real ones. It lets you know, even when you're not paying attention to it, that it is still there. For it to work, you have to be patient and quiet and trust that things will be okay in the darkness.

Not just okay. That there will be a way to find joy and to come out on top when everything around is murky and scary. And it is invisibly anchored to someone on the shore who is watching out for it, and who sees its flicker of light in the darkness, and who waits for it to glow.

I wish my grandfather were still alive. God, I wish he were. But his passing has given me a final gift: a self-trust, even when I can't see my way in the dark. That's why I carry a Bobolight. That, and to remind me of a good man who loved me.

—Greg Beatty

The Hall of Mirrors

Trisha, reclining in a pink satin nightgown and matching robe, invited the picture of a passé movie queen. Cobalt half-moons under her eyes obscured her cheekbones, circumscribing black marbles inside tufted lashes. She was bloated from painkillers, among them morphine, the drug of last resort, and her skin had the waxed sheen of a woman who never saw the sun. I looked from the photographs that lined the fireplace mantel to the woman in the bed and back again. The woman in the pictures had the daintiness and strength of a dancer, petite and slender, yet fit and firm, with bone structure that defined haute couture, surrounded by family and friends—a startling dark beauty. All that was behind her now, the photos remnants of another, earlier life, before tragedy struck.

When my sister was eleven years old, an accident

with a golf club caused severe facial fractures requiring extensive surgeries. As Trisha grew, she suffered from severe headaches but was able to maintain a successful business and to devote herself to her husband. But by 1995, the pain had taken over her life. Numerous specialists were consulted and various treatments were administered, but she continued to weaken until in her mid-fifties she had become completely bedridden. Her husband left her. She existed in a land of limbo, stuck in a cycle of pain that made every day a torment. Neuropathic pain in her head and neck was so severe she had become hypersensitive to light and sound.

I read Trisha's mail to her, piles of cards and letters. I called in a manicurist, a massage therapist, a hairdresser—anything to help make her feel better. I was her nurse, but more important, I was her only sister and could not rest until we found someone, some way to help her. Over the years we flew to Chicago, New York, and Dallas seeking treatments. I followed new research studies, scoured the archives of medical libraries, consulted doctor after doctor. I promised I would never desert her. As she grew less able to care for herself, I hired extra help and round-the-clock nursing care. I encouraged her never to give up.

Then one day I heard about a dentist who had done wonders for people with chronic pain. By now my sister had a permanent intravenous PICC so the morphine could continually help to ease her suffering. We flew to New York and met with Dr. German. He was a kindly older gentleman, reassuring and gentle with my sister. I held her hand as he measured her jaw and alignment. They would make custom plates that would slowly realign her jawbones. Dr. German warned us that the first few weeks would be difficult and that her pain might even increase at first.

During Trisha's recovery, I spent nights with her when other nurses could not be there. I came over every day to check on her and made sure she had enough medicine. I rubbed her feet and her back to take her mind off of the pain. I told her anecdotes of my days, and buoyed her with good thoughts. "You will have your life back," I told her. "Don't give up." I don't know where she got the strength to go on, but she did, making me even more in awe of her. I don't know that I could have been as strong. My sister believed she had the will to overcome it all, that in the end she would succeed. I knew her faith in God was strong. We prayed together daily.

At first the treatments did not seem to help. If anything, her pain worsened. By the third week, though, I saw something I had not seen in more than five years. She had gotten out of bed by herself and was talking about looking through her closet to find something to wear. She never made it past a few hangers, but she was up and walking. My sister had experienced only a few moments of normalcy, but I clung to those moments as a divine sign. This was her time to heal. I could feel it.

Each successive week brought little triumphs: a soaking bath, an entire meal eaten, sitting up in bed together watching her favorite television show. One afternoon she was able to go for a swim.

I could scarcely let myself think about all of the life issues she would have to face when she returned to the real world. She missed her husband terribly. He had divorced her and was now with a woman who had been her friend. Trisha's poor body was bruised and broken from all the medicine and procedures over the years. What she needed most was to be able to look in the mirror and see the beautiful woman she had been before.

As she improved she needed less and less morphine. Slowly her lovely face reappeared. She returned to her normal size, and we laughed to see her trying on business suits again. Then one day, she announced we were going out to lunch. I waited downstairs for her anxiously. The woman who floated down the stairs was someone I had not seen in many years. How lovely she looked.

We lunched at her favorite bistro, and I smiled hearing her order for both of us in French. After we finished eating, she handed me an envelope. Inside was a lovely card inscribed:

My Dearest Sister,

You have given up seven years of your life to help me regain mine. You have lost holidays and memories I can never return. When the doctors said there was nothing more they could do, you never wavered in your determination. When I lost my husband and my job, you made sure I could keep my home. You cared for me as nurse, nurturer, therapist, accountant, housekeeper, chauffeur, and masseuse. Through it all you kept my spirits high and never complained.

Now it is my turn to care for you.

In the Versailles Palace there is a room called the Hall of Mirrors. In it the ladies of the royal court could admire their elaborate hairstyles and opulent gowns. For seven years I have been afraid to look in a mirror. No longer. You, my dear sister, have made all things possible.

Tucked into the card were two tickets to Paris. We had a marvelous time together in the City of Lights, but the brightest lights came from the love shining in my sister's eyes.

—*Nan Leslie*

Shuffle, Step

"Just try it again, Lizzie, you'll get it."

But Lizzie knew she wouldn't. She watched Miss Carol in the mirror and at her side. Her high-heeled gold shoes scraping the slippery floor, slower than before.

"Shuuuffle. Step," said Miss Carol. "Shuffle. Step."

Lizzie pointed her eyes at Miss Carol's feet. She made it look so easy.

"Keep trying, Lizzie. You can do it," said Miss Carol. "I know you can."

Lizzie took a deep breath. "Shuffle. Step. Shuffle. Step," she repeated. But her words danced out of step with her feet. And she almost fell.

Erika and Emily started to giggle. At least, Lizzie thought so. After all, Erika and Emily knew how to shuffle, step. With both feet. With no problem. Lizzie stole a peek at them in their matching black leotards. They wore hair bows the colors of Christmas and held hands when Miss Carol told everyone to choose a partner.

Lizzie was usually left standing alone. Waiting for Miss Carol to take her hand and pair it with another child's or hold it herself—which Lizzie liked best, especially when Miss Carol gave it a warm squeeze before saying, "Okay, Lizzie. You can dance with me."

Holding Miss Carol's hand, Lizzie didn't hear the giggles. She didn't hear her shoes tap out of step.

But today was not one of those days.

"Hurry and get in place, Lizzie," said Miss Carol. "We're going over our number for the revue."

The revue. Lizzie wasn't exactly sure what that was, but she had the feeling she wasn't going to like it very well. Miss Carol said they would have costumes and that part sounded okay to Lizzie. She never had a costume before. At least not a costume that she didn't wear at Halloween. She hoped her costume had fringe and sparkles.

"You know, girls," said Miss Carol, "When you're up onstage, I'm not going to be there to hold your hand."

Lizzie remembered what she wasn't going to like about the revue. She walked to her place in the line, at the end, and waited for the music to begin. She did not want to disappoint Miss Carol. So she tried again. *Shuffle. Step.*

Across town, at the Garden Center Care Facility, Elizabeth Patterson heard a polka playing in the distance. She sat in the steel chair that was now part of her life and tapped her good foot along the dull ivory floor. She thought of her last visit from her granddaughter, Lizzie.

"Grandma, they're going to get you up today," Lizzie had said, while piling her lap with cut-out magazine pictures pasted on construction paper and headlined and hearted with bright magic markers. "Carl is going to get you to try to walk."

To walk. Grandma Elizabeth folded her hands. The last time she remembered walking was in her yellow kitchen. She remembered waving out the window as the neighbors ran to catch the bus. She remembered picking up the sack of flour to make cookies. She remembered grabbing two eggs, the bottle of vanilla—then the top of the cupboard, as she began to fall.

What a mess I'm making, she remembered thinking.

"C'mon, Miss Elizabeth, easy does it," said Carl, as his burly arms pulled her up to her feet. Carl smelled like pizza and had a laugh that some people might think was a little too loud, but Grandma Elizabeth liked him just fine.

"All you have to do is slide one foot forward, then set it down easy," said Carl, positioning her arms just right on the narrow bar of the metal walker.

Grandma Elizabeth tried to match his smile but settled on a nod.

She gripped the walker with her shaking hands and took a deep breath. *Slide one foot forward, then set it down easy,* she thought. But even her silent words danced out of step with her feet. And she almost fell.

Mrs. Bowman and Mabel Pratt started to giggle. At least, Grandma Elizabeth thought so. They had every right. After all, Mrs. Bowman and Mabel Pratt knew how to walk. Without their chairs. Without a problem. Grandma Elizabeth stole a peek at them in their flowered dusters. They wore cotton candy hairdos the colors of the sky and sat by each other each night at supper.

Grandma Elizabeth usually ate alone in her room. Waiting for Carl to take her chair and roll it by another in the large dining hall or stay there with her—which Grandma Elizabeth liked best, especially when Carl brought her a treat from the kitchen, like Jell-O with extra whipped cream. But it was not time for dessert.

"You can do it, Miss Elizabeth. I know you can," Carl said, his voice pulling her toward the long hallway.

She did not want to disappoint him. So she tried again. *Slide one foot forward, then set it down easy.*

Weeks passed as Lizzie and Grandma Elizabeth both practiced their new steps. They stood each night, in front of their mirrors, when no one was watching, when no one was holding their hands. They each tried to do their best. For Miss Carol and for Carl. But mostly for each other.

And every day it got a little easier, and a little better . . . all the way to showtime.

"Now, smile, Lizzie, and wait for the flash," said Miss Carol.

Lizzie tried her best to keep her eyes forward, but they were pulled by dozens of girls and mothers, all hairsprayed and glittery. They zigzagged from the dressing room to the bathroom, to the drinking fountain and the windows, using up all the extra energy charged for Miss Carol's School of Dance's twelfth annual revue.

Grandma Elizabeth was excited, too.

"Don't you look like a picture," said Carl walking into her room. "Who's the lucky fella?" he asked, giving her soft shoulder an affectionate squeeze.

She smiled and held up the invitation from Lizzie. And Carl understood.

"Well, you sure look lovely," he said.

Grandma Elizabeth thought so, too. She'd had the beautician fix her hair special and put polish on her nails. Peach. To match her new dress. Lizzie had picked it out, saying it would be just perfect.

"Okay," said Miss Carol, "You're up next."

Lizzie stood behind the big red curtain, looking down at her shiny gold shoes and then up at her folded hands, fingernails painted peach to match her costume. The fringe on her skirt swished as she scooted to her position in line, walking quietly and carefully as Miss Carol had instructed during rehearsal. The lights caught the sparkle on her sleeves, and she watched it flicker on the shiny surface of the stage. She heard her heart beat. One, two, three. One, two, three. Then the whisper of Miss Carol, "You can do it." *Shuffle. Step.* Lizzie took a deep breath and smiled.

As the music began, Elizabeth Patterson was breathing deeply and smiling, too. The walk down the aisle was long. But she made it. Her daughter at her side, Carl in her head, Lizzie in her heart. *You can do it,* she said to herself. *Just slide one foot forward, then set it down easy.*

She found her own rhythm as she sat, front row, tapping her good foot and following the sparkle of the moment as it reflected from the stage. One step at a time.

—*Judi Christy*

 Gordon

I was eleven when I first met Gordon. My mother and father had been divorced only a matter of days, so I wasn't a prime candidate for meeting Mother's new beau. I treated him rudely despite the gifts he brought to me. I didn't want anything to do with anyone who might stand in the way of what I knew would be an imminent reconciliation between my parents.

At fourteen I gained a stepfather. Gordon and my mother married after a three-year, turbulent courtship. By that time I had come to realize I was gaining an ally right in my own home. Gordon didn't always agree with my mother's method of discipline. He, in fact, believed that children were interesting smaller versions of adults, and regarded their feelings and thoughts with an honesty and respect that I had never known.

Learning to accept him into my home and my heart brought me experiences I would have forgone otherwise. Gordon was understanding and appreciative of my love of the theater, and he carted me back and forth to rehearsals, productions, and cast parties. He even let me have a cast party at our house. He cooked for two days, set up an elaborate feast, and stayed upstairs while my friends and I indulged in sheer delight. When they went home, Gordon came back downstairs and cleaned the mess himself, sending me to bed.

"You worked hard," he said, referring to my part in the school play. "You need to go to bed."

He encouraged my friendships, and was one of those parents who constantly chauffeured groups of kids to dances and ball games. We'd pile into the back of his beat-up Datsun pickup truck, covered with blankets, as he delivered all of my friends to their homes.

After enduring a childhood full of conflict with my mother, I reached a point one spring when I decided I'd prefer to go live with my biological father. Knowing I would meet staunch opposition from my mother, I instead approached Gordon with my plan.

"I hate to see you go," he said. "But your happiness is what's important here."

As it turned out, my father wasn't able to have me come and live with him. Sadly, this caused a rift in my relationship with him. I was truly disappointed but at the same time bolstered by the fact that Gordon had put my wishes and needs ahead of anyone else's, including his own. This concept was new to me, but one I came to accept throughout my years with him.

When I married young and found myself in a dire financial situation, he loaned me money but never made me feel like I'd imposed. He became "Grandpa Gordon" to my children. When my marriage failed, he encouraged and stood by me, and never once said, "I told you so."

Years later—and since divorced from my mother—Gordon walked me down the aisle a second time, and welcomed more grandchildren. All the while he remained my rock and my strongest parental guide. He met and married Carol, a wonderful woman, and they've since spent many happy years together.

Gordon has never once in more than three decades said a negative word about my "real" father. In fact, he consistently encouraged our visits and praised his efforts. When my sister got married, both Gordon and Dad walked her down the aisle. With Gordon's blessing, both my sister and I have re-established our relationships with our father.

Throughout history, countless philosophers have contended that "blood runs thicker than water." I beg to differ. Although I love my natural father dearly, I have another father not of my blood and no longer through marriage who has stood by me through thick and thin. He has taught me some of life's most valuable lessons. He remains my confidant and true friend. And he is my closest "relative."

From petulant preteen years through adulthood, I have had the honor of learning from this brilliant psychologist and professor. Yet none of the knowledge I've acquired from Gordon touches on his profession. I gained, instead, insight into what really matters in this life, and I learned that families are there to help us live it.

What did Gordon learn from all of this? That's hard to say. If I was to fathom a guess, it would go something like a quote I've seen on greeting cards and wall hangings. It reads, "A hundred years from now it won't matter what kind of car I drove or how much money was in my bank account. What will matter is that I was important in the life of a child."

I was that child.

—*Kimberly Ripley*

Ambassadors Are Everywhere

Yesterday I met one of our country's outstanding ambassadors. He was dressed informally, and had an outgoing and easy manner. He was actually hanging out with his mother at a print shop, and when he saw me making copies, he hurried over.

"Can I press the button for you?" he asked. His smile was as welcoming as the first star, and his attitude was helpful and eager.

"Sure," I told him.

He had to stand on tiptoe. He pressed the button, and a copy emerged.

"Can I do it again?" he asked politely, bouncing slightly.

"Of course," I told him.

The ambassador's mother looked over from her copy machine.

"Aaron," she cautioned, "Be polite."

I assured her I wanted his help. All too soon, my copies were finished. But the ambassador wasn't going to let me leave the shop all serious and weighed down with a bunch of businessy-looking black-and-white papers. He was going to cheer and entertain me by showing me his dinosaur sticker collection. He counted each sticker, in a free-form fashion, and wasn't a bit rigid about not including every single number in the traditional order. He showed me the fiercest dinosaurs, the ones he was personally a little afraid of, and he pointed out the ones he wanted to collect himself.

"Any more buttons you need pressed?" he asked, when the viewing was complete.

"Not this time," I said regretfully. I shook his hand and thanked him for his help. I smiled at his lucky mom and went off, feeling happy and cheerful. The ambassador had worked his magic.

That evening, I met another ambassador on my walk. She was practicing hitting a softball in her front yard. As I passed, she made a mighty hit.

"Wow," she said, "I did it! Did you see that?" she asked me.

"It was an amazing hit," I said. "Were you surprised?"

"No," she said. "I'm good. I just can't aim it in the right direction." She smiled and ran off to collect the ball.

As I walked, I thought about a hitter who had no sense of direction. For some, that could ruin a game. But this ambassador was obviously a master at concentrating on talents and downplaying challenges. She knew how to get pleasure from what was good.

Back in my office, I surveyed the work I had done that day. I picked up my red pen and started editing. Then I thought of the softball-playing ambassador. I took a blue pen and circled the phrases I really liked first.

In these days of turmoil and confusion, I am grateful for the many fine, highly trained ambassadors that are serving here and abroad. These ambassadors are renowned for their social and interpersonal skills, for astute evaluations of delicate matters, for their creative problem-solving abilities. These ambassadors also have a level of sophistication and respect for protocol that is quite appropriate to their prestigious political stations.

These days, when we are so worn and worried, maybe we need even more than those auspicious skills. What if we supplemented our diplomatic team with a small squirmy band of unschooled ambassadors, those who are still learning to count and still think everything counts? These high-energy live-wire kids could go beyond protocol and polite expression and eagerly connect with any willing person. These kids are already at work in grocery stores, shoe stores, and front yards. They weave their magic by drawing you in, whether you deserve it or not.

What if the ambassador from the copy shop in Kansas City got to play with the ambassador from a fish market in Tokyo? What if the ambassador from urban Chicago got to connect with an ambassador from the cocoa fields of Ghana? What if, in addition to seeing national news about strategies and stalemates, we simply saw footage of our ambassadors playing together? Of course, there would be occasional skirmishes, squabbles, and squeals. But I have confidence that, left to their own devices, our ambassadors would figure it all out.

Every day, we are confronted with political dilemmas, corporate scandals, global fears. We live in the presence of crime, conflict, and war. These new ambassadors could be our guides in solving some of these problems. Before we make our decisions, we could simply look down at the eager smiles and hopeful faces of these children, ready to forget all the things that make us different, ready to reach out and bring us all together.

—*Deborah H. Shouse*

A Five-Dollar Bill

I t was the third week in December, and I was writing out my charity checks. I had intended to write fewer checks that year, because I wasn't working and had definitely decided that charity begins at home—my home.

However, when I counted up the number of checks, I was shocked. Instead of fewer, there were more. For a moment, I was tempted to tear up a couple of envelopes, but I couldn't. Once I'd sealed the envelope, it was as if I had given my word, and I don't like to go back on my word. So, I mailed them all and patted myself on the back for being such a "charitable" person.

But I didn't feel charitable. I felt grumpy. Why? Maybe because I do it all at once, so it feels like a lot of money. Maybe because the amount grows every year, because more people are in need. Or maybe it's simply because my back hurts after sitting in one position for such a long time. Whatever the reason, I walked around for a few days like a bear that has been woken up in the middle of winter. Definitely not someone you wanted to tangle with.

Then something happened that opened my eyes and gave me the swift kick in the pants I needed. While I complain about donating to charity, the truth is, I can afford to. Even though I wasn't working that year, I had been able to save money over the years and certainly wasn't destitute. If things got bad, I knew I would be able to go back to work, at least part time.

In the meantime, although I buy a lot of my clothes secondhand and may not go out to fancy restaurants, I live in a house and I always have money to put food on the table and to pay the heating bill. Giving to charity means fewer frills for me, but that's what they really are—frills.

I can afford to give to charity and I do, but not until it hurts. Then I met a woman who did give until it hurt. And I felt ashamed of myself. She didn't set out to shame me, any more than she set out to be a knight in shining armor to a homeless man.

All she wanted was a hamburger.

I discovered her on a Web site we were both writing for. I was a veteran, which in cyber-time meant I had been there for several months; she was a newbie. I had read a few of her stories and liked their humor and honesty.

But when I saw one of her stories, "That Time of Month," I almost passed it by. My first reaction was that she was writing about . . . well, a time of month all women are familiar with.

For some reason, I decided to read it, anyway. That's when I found out "that time of month" is when the money from one disability check is gone and the month still has a few days left. When lunch is watery tea, a few crackers, and maybe half a can of bargain-basement tuna fish when you hate tuna fish. And when dinner is the other half of the can without the crackers.

Then you remember the five-dollar bill you managed to save for just such a time, when the thought of eating tuna fish makes you gag. Feeling incredibly rich, you decide to splurge on dinner out. Not at a four-star restaurant, but at McDonald's. Forget the truffles; all you want is a hamburger with all the fixings. If you don't order fries and a drink, you'll even have some change to put away for another month, another hamburger.

Instead of taking your purse, you just slip the money in a book you got at the Salvation Army store for a quarter and will now return so someone else can enjoy it, though not before you take out the money, of course. Then you get dressed and, clutching the book, painfully walk down the stairs and begin the slow, two-block trip to McDonald's.

As you cut through an alley, you notice a bundle of rags. You peer closer. The rags turn into a man huddled against a building. He looks at you and half smiles. You clutch the book a little tighter, but he doesn't look that frightening.

You smile back a little tentatively but continue walking. Your thoughts are on that burger, now just a short block away.

Then you stop. Suddenly, the burger, the same burger that just a minute ago meant everything to you, doesn't seem important now. You turn around and hand the book, complete with your last five dollars, to the raggedy man, telling him you hope he enjoys it. He looks at you for a moment, and then quietly thanks you.

You return home, trying to convince yourself that tuna isn't that bad, not when you can eat it inside a warm apartment, knowing you will have a bed to sleep in that night.

The story was told matter-of-factly, just another day in the life of someone. There was no patting herself on the back for being such a good person. No complaining about the hard life she was living.

I was so impressed, I did two things. One, I put a link in one of my articles so anyone who read it would know about her story and could easily click on it. Since we got paid a couple of pennies per click, I hoped the extra readers would translate into another burger to make up for the one she'd lost. And two, I e-mailed her to tell her how much I had enjoyed her article.

A day later she e-mailed me to thank me for the link. I e-mailed her to tell her she was welcome. Then she e-mailed me to comment on one of my stories. I e-mailed her to comment on one of hers.

Since then, we've moved from talking about writing to talking about ourselves. Through little snippets she's told me and stories she's written about her experiences, I've come to realize what a remarkable woman she truly is. Not that she would ever say that about herself. So I'll say it for her.

Having battled, and continuing to battle, major medical problems and depression, she has somehow found the strength to reach out to others. She has learned to find joy in small things and to teach others to do the same. If you're stuck in a wheelchair, decorate it. If you've lost a breast to cancer, write a story about your parrot eating the prosthesis, so others can smile. If you have only five dollars, give it away and enrich two lives—yours and that of the person who receives it.

I would like to say that knowing her has made me a better, more generous person, another Mother Theresa, and that I, too, would give away my last five dollars. But I know myself better than that. I know

I'd hang on to my last five dollars with every ounce of strength I had.

Still, though I'm certainly no saint, I've begun to take one or two tentative steps toward being that better, more generous person. These days, if I give spare change to street people a little more often or don't grumble quite as much when I write charity checks, I know why. It all started when a woman gave her last five dollars to someone she didn't know and created a ripple effect ending hundreds of miles away—with me.

—*Harriet Cooper*

Tell Your Story in the Next *Cup of Comfort*!

We hope you have enjoyed *A Cup of Comfort for Inspiration* and that you will share it with all the special people in your life.

We're brewing up lots of other *Cup of Comfort* books, each filled to the brim with true stories that will touch your heart and soothe your soul. The inspiring tales included in these collections are written by everyday men and women, and we would love to include one of your stories in an upcoming edition of *A Cup of Comfort*.

Do you have a powerful story about an experience that dramatically changed or enhanced your life? A compelling story that can stir our emotions, make us think, and bring us hope? An inspiring story that reveals lessons of humility within a vividly told tale? Tell us your story!

Each *Cup of Comfort* contributor will receive a monetary fee, author credit, and a complimentary copy of the book. Just e-mail your submission of 1,000 to 2,000 words (one story per e-mail; no attachments, please) to:

cupofcomfort@adamsmedia.com

Or, if e-mail is unavailable to you, send it to:

A Cup of Comfort
Adams Media Corporation
57 Littlefield Street
Avon, Massachusetts 02322

You can submit as many stories as you'd like, for whichever volumes you'd like. Make sure to include your name, address, and other contact information. We also welcome your suggestions or stories for new *Cup of Comfort* themes.

For more information, please visit our Web site: *www.cupofcomfort.com*.

We look forward to sharing many more soothing *Cups of Comfort* with you!

 Contributors

Beth Rothstein Ambler ("One Man and a Whole Lot of Somebodies") resides in New Jersey with her husband, Chuck, and her two canine companions. She enjoys the luxury of pursuing her hobby of writing short stories, one of which was published in *A Cup of Comfort for Women*.

Shery Ma Belle Arrieta ("Close Encounters of the Best Kind") works full-time from her home in Laguna, Philippines, as a writer, online writing workshop facilitator, Internet development consultant to businesses and organizations, and Web site designer. She is the founder of e-Writer's Place.

Nancy Baker ("Recipe for Life") resides in College Station, Texas, with her husband of forty-five years and two cats. She retired from Texas A&M University, where she was a program coordinator and trainer. Since then, she has pursued her lifelong love of writing and has been published in national magazines and anthologies, including *A Cup of Comfort for Friends* and *A Cup of Comfort for Women*. She is currently working on her grandmother's biography.

William M. Barnes ("I Won't Forget"), a retired geologist, has been writing for six years. He has received numerous awards for his essays, short stories, and novels, and has had several pieces published in anthologies and in *The Houston Chronicle*. He lives in the Woodlands, Texas, where he is a member of the Woodlands Writers Guild.

Greg Beatty ("Why I Carry a Bobolight") lives in the Pacific Northwest, where he spends time with his girlfriend, writes, teaches for the University of Phoenix Online, and tries to stay out of the rain. One of his many published stories appears in *A Cup of Comfort for Friends*.

Marcia E. Brown ("Over the Hill") is an Austin, Texas, senior citizen whose writing has appeared in magazines, newspapers, and anthologies. Specializing in humor, she has completed a book of her funniest family stories. Marcia is a member of the National League of American Pen Women and the Texas Writers' League.

Christy Caballero ("Practical Magic") is a freelance writer and photographer living in the Pacific Northwest. She writes about wildlife and matters of the heart for magazines, newspapers, and rescue groups. Her special bond with animals began with Honcho, the massive German shepherd who decided she belonged to him the day after she was born in Anchorage, Alaska.

Judi Christy ("Shuffle, Step") is an Ohio freelance writer who has penned hundreds of scripts, speeches, and short stories as well as a book on local history. Judi is an arts advocate and antique collector who enjoys good laughs, good wines, and the good company of her family, friends, and fictional acquaintances. Her stories have appeared in other volumes of the *Cup of Comfort* series.

Harriet Cooper ("A Five-Dollar Bill") is a freelance humorist and essayist living in Toronto, Ontario, Canada. Her stories, poems, articles, and anecdotes have appeared in a wide range of newspapers, magazines, anthologies, and Web sites. When not writing, she teaches English as a second language, practices yoga, and hides from her three cats.

Binsey Coté ("With a Little Boost from My Friends") is the mother of four children and has been married to her high school sweetheart for twenty-three years. She currently works as a professional doula, assisting couples throughout their pregnancy, labor, and postpartum. She resides in Santa Maria, California.

Gina Daggett ("Keep Walking") is a freelance writer living in Portland, Oregon. She's an in-house writer for *Nervy Girl*, as well as a regular contributor to *Just Out* and the *Portland Tribune*. Her work has also appeared in *Girlfriends*, *Lesbian News*, and *Kerf*. She reads for *Tin House* literary journal and is a long-distance runner.

Jean Davidson ("The Greatest Man I Hardly Knew") is an "adventurer," who at the "young age of fifty-nine" recently enrolled as a full-time university student in

Pocatello, Idaho, "just for the fun of it." Her greatest passions are being with her family and writing their stories.

Marty Dodge ("The Connection") was born, raised, and continues to live with her husband, Dave, and golden retriever, Casey, in the northeast corner of Iowa. The couple has two children and one grandson, and since retirement have traveled extensively throughout North America. After a rewarding thirty-year career as a voice and piano teacher, she is pursuing a lifetime love of writing. This is her first published piece.

John Forrest ("Ruthie's Run") retired after thirty-four years as an educator and began writing about the exceptional events and wonderful people that have enriched his life. His stories have been published in several magazines and on CBC Radio's "First Person Singular." He lives with his wife, Carol, in Orillia, Ontario, Canada, where they enjoy golfing, traveling, and meddling in the lives of their grown children Rob and Diana.

Brenda Fritsvold ("Incidental Kin") lives in Seattle, Washington, with her husband and two young sons.

Danielle R. Gibbings ("The Picture on the Wall") is a mother of two, wife, full-time university student, part-time supervisor, and freelance writer in Winnipeg, Manitoba, Canada. She has published fiction and poetry in various literary e-zines and writes articles and book reviews for a local newspaper. Danielle is powered by an equal balance of friends, caffeine, and family.

Dawn Goldsmith ("Snow Angel"), newspaper reporter, bibliophile, and Illinois resident, freelances full-time and has published essays and articles in a variety of publications and online sites, including *Christian Science Monitor, Skirt! Magazine, Quilt World*, and several anthologies. She also reviews books for *Publishers Weekly* and *Crescent Blues E'magazine*.

Kathryn Gore ("Warm Hearts in a Cold Winter") lives in Magna, Utah. She is a wife and mother of nine children, ranging in age from four years to twenty-four years. She enjoys time spent with her family and in church service. In her spare time she loves to write, read, craft, and sew.

Nancy Gustafson ("The Salvation of Jan and Kurt") has published poetry, short fiction, essays, and articles in several anthologies and journals. She is retired from Sam Houston State University, where she worked as a program coordinator for the Correctional Management Institute of Texas. She lives with her husband, Jan, in Huntsville, Texas.

Tracey Henry ("Balance") is a writer residing in the Tampa Bay area. Her work has appeared in several publications. She also writes a regular column for Backwash.com. She and her husband have two young sons. This story is dedicated to them, to Diane and Sandy, and to the amazing boys of Attention Home.

Joyce Holt ("Angel Wings"), a native and resident of Seattle, Washington, wrote the script for the city of Renton's centennial pageant, a two-hour musical chronicle of local history. She likes to weave, draw caricatures, perform ventriloquism, volunteer in church children's programs, and write science fiction and historical-fantasy novels.

Amy Jenkins ("Sisters in Time") writes articles and creative nonfiction, and is widely published in magazines and books and has read her work on public radio. A lover of anthologies, she manages Anthologies Online, and her work has appeared in several compilations. She lives in Wisconsin with her husband, children, and pets.

Sandy Keefe ("Doll Cake") enjoys a rich and wonderfully balanced life in El Dorado Hills, California, as the mother of three (Burl, Shannon, and Allie). She works as a nurse case manager for children with special needs and writes professional articles, online continuing education programs, and inspirational short stories. Sandy's stories have also appeared in *A Cup of Comfort Cookbook*, *A Cup of Comfort for Women*, and *A Cup of Comfort for Friends*.

Charles Langley ("Reglar Feller") returned to writing after a fifty-nine-year hiatus and at age eighty-six has published more than 100 stories, poems, articles, and columns for e-zines, print magazines, and books. He recently compiled an anthology of the writings of members of the Creative Writing Group, which he moderates.

Nan Leslie ("The Hall of Mirrors") writes full-time from her lakeside cottage in Maine. Her award-winning fiction has been widely published, and she currently edits two literary journals and is working on her first novel.

Norma Lewis ("Gotta Keep Paddling"), a former accounting and sales professional, has been a freelance writer since 1991. She has published more than 100 magazine articles and one nonfiction juvenile book. Widowed from her beloved husband in 1999, she now lives with her cat in Spring Lake, Michigan, where she dotes on her two grandchildren.

Peggy MacKay ("The Dollar Dance") sells real estate for Coldwell Banker in Buena Vista, Colorado. A former account executive for AT&T, she later designed and facilitated outdoor experiential programs for corporate clients. Peggy is a lifelong explorer of the human condition; her avocation is writing.

Valerie L. Merahn ("The Journey of Jake and Dora") graduated cum laude from American University in Washington, D.C. She now lives in New York City, where she is the vice president and general manager of NewsExpress, a division of Burrelle's Information Services. In her spare time, Valerie enjoys writing and is currently working on a collection of children's stories.

Susan B. Mitchell ("Corinna's Quilts"), Corinna's aunt, was born and raised in Provo, Utah, where she fell in love with Robert Mitchell. "Our wedding was delayed because my mother was expecting a new baby," she says. "Mary, the new baby sister, grew up to be Corinna's mommy." The Mitchells enjoy nine children, eighteen grandchildren, and oodles of nieces and nephews. Susan is also a contributor to A *Cup of Comfort Cookbook*.

Sharon Nesbit ("Prince of Paupers") lives in Troutdale, Oregon, and has worked as a columnist and reporter for the *Gresham Outlook* newspaper for more than thirty years. She is an amateur historian and author of a small book on the history of Edgefield Manor.

Janice Lane Palko ("Willed"), a writing instructor at a local community college and a columnist, has more than seventy-five published works. She resides in Pittsburgh, Pennsylvania, with her husband and three children. Currently, she is busy dreaming up a compelling plot and memorable characters for her third novel.

Michelle Peters ("Give Your Heart Away") resides in Winnipeg, Manitoba, Canada, with her husband and young son. Currently on maternity leave from a social work position, she is considering pursuing a career in writing. This is her first published work.

Kimberly Ripley ("A Bartender's Story" and "Gordon") makes her home in New Hampshire with her husband, Roland, and five children. She is the author of five books, including *Freelancing Later in Life*, and conducts writing workshops around the country. Her writing has been published in magazines and anthologies, including several volumes of the *Cup of Comfort* series.

Julie Clark Robinson's ("The Gift of Robin") muse is usually her family. Much to their relief, she has changed subjects in her current project, a self-help book titled *You, Too, Can Be Downright Giddy*. Her writing has appeared in *Family Circle, Bride's, The Plain Dealer Sunday Magazine*, and in anthologies, including *A Cup of Comfort for Women*. The Robinsons live in Hudson, Ohio.

Leigh P. Rogers ("For the Love of Pixie") is a writer whose stories have been published in *Spies' Wives* and *Nudges from God*. She was raised all over the world as the daughter of a CIA agent and is currently working on a manuscript about her experiences abroad. She now resides in Benicia, California.

Marjorie Rommel ("The Last Long Wave Good-bye") lives in Auburn, Washington. A newspaper reporter and editor for many years, she now works as a media relations consultant and college instructor. She was a 2000 Willard R. Espy Literary Foundation resident and received an Adam Family Foundation White Bridge Traveling Fellowship in 2001. She has a husband, six kids, tons of grandkids, a fistful of greatgrands, a dog named Toby Glass, and a cat named Harry.

Marcia Rudoff ("Begin Again") teaches memoir writing at the Bainbridge Island Senior Community Center and writes a monthly column for the *Bainbridge Review*. When not marveling at how much more time volunteering takes than working and raising a family, she enjoys writing, spending time with family and friends, baseball, and chocolate. Her award-winning essays have appeared in *Northwest Runner*, the *Seattle Times,* and *Stories with Grace.*

Nancy Scott ("So I Ask You") is an essayist and poet with numerous credits in regional and national publications, including *ByLine, Dialogue,* and *The Philadelphia Inquirer.* Her writing has also been published in the anthology *Staring Back* and in *A Cup of Comfort for Women.*

Deborah H. Shouse ("Sweet Moments" and "Ambassadors Are Everywhere") loves to write about the extraordinary nature of everyday life. She is a writer, speaker, editor, and creativity catalyst. Her work has appeared in *Reader's Digest, Newsweek, Woman's Day, Family Circle,* and *Ms.* She has written several business books and memoirs, including *Making Your Message Memorable: Communicating Through Stories.*

Linda Sonna ("Here and Now, If Not Always") is a psychologist, college instructor, poet, and author of five parenting books, including *The Everything® Tween Book, The Everything® Potty Training Book,* and *The Everything® Toddler Book.* She lives in Taos, New Mexico, where she writes and counsels clients. She has fostered six children.

Joyce Stark ("The Gloved Guitarist of Tossa de Mar") was born and lives in northeast Scotland, and works as a business manager for a mortgage broker. She and her husband love touring Europe and the United States, where Joyce stuffs her pockets with notes for stories to write later.

Kelly L. Stone ("Power Ball of Love") is a writer and a licensed professional counselor who has worked in the field of children's mental health for more than thirteen years. Her essays have been published in *A Cup of Comfort for Mothers & Daughters* and other anthologies. She lives in the Atlanta area with her four dogs and three cats.

Mary Stripling ("Errands of Honor") has received awards for poetry and prose. She and her husband of forty-two years have two grown children. A registered nurse, she spends her leisure time gardening, reading, and enjoying family and friends.

Anna Therien ("Passing the Halo") lives east of Toronto, Canada, with her husband, two children, and five spoiled cats. When she isn't writing or pursuing the elusive halo, she runs a marketing company with her husband and volunteers on the board of directors of the Writer's Circle of Durham Region.

April Thompson ("Strawberries"), a San Francisco–based freelance journalist, writes for such magazines as

Hope, The Sun, Natural Home, and *Via*. She is currently in Conakry, Guinea, working as a reporter for the United Nations World Food Programme.

Roberta B. Updegraff ("Roots for Sofia") has been happily married to her high school sweetheart for thirty years and is the mother of three terrific children. She is a freelance writer and substitute teacher for Williamsport Area School District in Pennsylvania. She is the author of six Church Choir Mysteries and writes for Presbyterian Disaster Assistance's *Mosaic* magazine.

Sue Vitou ("The Wonder of Now") is an award-winning writer of more than 200 published articles. Her work has appeared in *The Plain Dealer, Sun Newspapers, The Medina Gazette, A Cup of Comfort for Women*, and other publications. She lives in Medina, Ohio, with her four children: Matt, John, Brad, and Brenna.

Adrian R. Ward ("To Hold and Behold") is a full-time writer and mother of four young children. Her writing is inspired by her faith, her southern heritage, and her adventures in parenting. She and her husband, Wes, are raising their family in Springville, Alabama.

Barbara Whitby ("For Sura, Who Claimed Her Need to Be Touched"), is a native of England, lives by the sea in Halifax, in eastern Canada. Now retired, she hikes, sails, belly dances, acts as a film extra, and enjoys life as a great-grandmother. Through writing and the occasional radio broadcast, she shares an ardent interest in history, spirituality, healing, and travel.

Gila Zalon ("Stopping Traffic"), the mother of three grown children, divides her time between managing her husband's law office, writing, and acting in local theater groups. When her children were young, she wrote two plays for school fundraisers in which she also performed, and more recently she wrote two short screenplays that were produced by a local film company. With "Stopping Traffic," Gila is thrilled to have entered the world of books.

Kim Zarzour ("When All Is Said") is a freelance writer whose works have been published in national magazines and aired on radio. A former reporter with several daily newspapers, she is the author of parenting books, including *Facing the Schoolyard Bully: How to Raise an Assertive Child in an Aggressive World*. She cares for her three children, a golden retriever, several half-dead goldfish, and her long-suffering husband in their home near Toronto, Canada.

About the Editor

Colleen Sell has long believed in the power of story to connect us with our inner spirits, the Higher Spirit, and one another. Her passion for storytelling has been inspired and nurtured by many mentors and teachers, a gift she is paying forward by encouraging and helping others to share their stories.

The editor of more than fifty published books, Colleen has also coauthored and ghostwritten several books, including *10-Minute Zen* (2002). She is the former editor-in-chief of two award-winning consumer magazines, and has been a columnist, essayist, and journalist.

She lives with her husband in a nineteenth-century Victorian on a forty-acre lavender and tree farm in the Pacific Northwest, where she continues to write tales both tall and true.